Welcome to Amsterdam!

This opening fold-out contains a general map of Amsterdam to help you
visualise the 6 large districts discussed in this guide, and 4 pages of valuable
information, handy tips and useful addresses.

Discover Amsterdam through 6 districts and 6 maps

A Centraal Station / Nieuwmarkt / Dam / Spui

B Western islands / Jordaan / Northern canals

C Southern canals / Singel / Leidseplein

D Southern canals / Rembrandtplein / Amstel

E Vondelpark / Museumplein / De Pijp

F Waterlooplein / Plantage / Oosterdok

For each district there is a double-page of addresses (restaurants – listed in
ascending order of price – pubs, bars, music venues and shops) followed by
a fold-out map for the relevant area with the essential places to see (indicated
on the map by a star ★). These places are by no means all that Amsterdam has
to offer but to us they are unmissable. The grid-referencing system (**A** B2)
makes it easy for you to pinpoint addresses quickly on the map.

Transport and hotels in Amsterdam

The last fold-out consists of a transport map and 4 pages of practical
information that include a selection of hotels.

Thematic index

Lists all the adresses, sites and monuments mentioned in this guide.

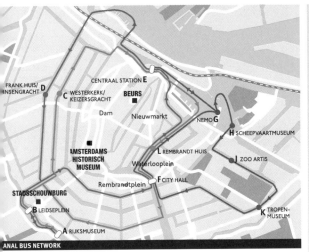

Within the map:
- FRANK HUIS/INSENGRACHT **D**
- CENTRAAL STATION **E**
- WESTERKERK/KEIZERSGRACHT **C**
- BEURS
- Dam
- Nieuwmarkt
- NEMO **G**
- SCHEEPVAARTMUSEUM **H**
- AMSTERDAMS HISTORISCH MUSEUM
- Waterlooplein
- **L** REMBRANDT HUIS
- ZOO ARTIS **J**
- Rembrandtplein
- **F** CITY HALL
- STADSSCHOUWBURG
- **B** LEIDSEPLEIN
- TROPEN-MUSEUM **K**
- **A** RIJKSMUSEUM
- ANAL BUS NETWORK

...ty offer guided tours.
n roller skates
oin up with 2,000 skaters
n Fridays in front of the
lmmuseum (**E** A1) for a
ighttime tour of the city.
kates can also be rented
ear the side entrance to the
'ondelpark
Amstelveenseweg).

AMSTERDAM
OR FREE

Classical music
Muziektheater (Stopera)
(**A** C3)
→ Amstel 3
Tel. 551 81 00
Oct-May: Tue 12.30–1pm
Concertgebouw (**E** B2)
→ Tel. 671 83 45
Sep-June: Wed 12.30–1pm
Clocktower concerts
Munttoren
→ Fri noon–1pm
Westerkerk
→ Tue noon–1pm
Oude Kerk
→ Sat 4–5pm

Zuiderkerk
→ Thu noon–1pm
**Civil Guard
Museum** (**A** A4)
→ Adjoining the Historical
Museum
Seventeenth-century
paintings in the open street.

MUSEUMS

Opening hours
May vary. Museums
generally open later on
Sunday (11am–1pm).
Reductions
These vary for under-18s,
are systematic for over-65s,
but rare for students.
Amsterdam Pass
→ Ticket includes transport
and entrance to 25 museums:
see the Transportation pages
MJK (Museumjaarkaart)
→ At the VVV and museums
Price 25 € (12.50 € for
under-25s).
Free admission to
400 museums in Holland,
valid for one year.

Free admission
→ end April (info at Uitburo)
During the national
museum weekend.

SHOPPING

Opening hours
Mon noon–6pm; Tue-Sat
9am–6pm (5pm Sat) and, in
the center, Sun noon–5pm.
Late-night opening
→ Thu 9pm
Annual closing
→ Dec 25–26 , Jan 1,
April 30, May 5
Department stores
Metz & Co (**C** C4)
→ Keizersgracht 455
Tel. 520 70 20
Maison de la
Bonneterie (**A** B4)
→ Rokin 140 Tel. 531 34 00
Commercial center
Magna Plaza (**A** A3)
→ Nieuwezijds
Voorburgwaal 182
Tel. 626 91 99
Located in a former neo-
Gothic-style post office.

INDENTED GABLE

CITY PROFILE

- 735,000 inhabitants
- 145 nationalities
- 550,000 bicycles
- 9 clock towers ■ 165 canals ■ 42 museums
- 6,800 listed buildings
- 1,402 cafés
- 14 million visitors per year

RIVERBOAT

THE 'HOFJES'

Jordaan abounds in these 18th-century Beguine convents and hospices, their hidden courtyards bedecked with flowers. Only the **Begijnhof (A A5)** is officially open to the public, so discretion is called for.

'T Venetiae Hofje (C B2)
→ Elandsstraat 104–142
Sint Andrieshofje (B A5)
→ Egelantiersgracht 107
Anslohofje (B B5)
→ Egelantierstraat 50
Van Brienenhofje (B B5)
→ Prinsengracht 89–133
Lindenhofje (B B4)
→ Lindengracht 94–112
Suyckerhofje (B B4)
→ Lindengracht 149–163

USEFUL INFO

Calling Amsterdam from abroad
Dial international code + 31 (for Holland) + 20 (for Amsterdam) + number (7 figures).
Calling abroad from Amsterdam
Dial 00 + country code + number (without initial 0).
Tourist offices (VVV)
Tel. 0900 400 40 40
The Amsterdam Tourist Office has four outlets: at Stationsplein 10; Centraal Station; Leidseplein 1; and in Shiphol Airport
Useful numbers
Police, fire service
→ *112*
Medical center
→ *0900 503 20 42*

WWW.

Amsterdam online
→ *www.amsterdam.nl*
Information in English on

events, restaurants, etc.
→ *www.simplyamsterdam.nl*
→ *www.amsterdam.info*
In English; Internet links on museums, hotels, etc.
Internet cafés
EasyInternetCafé
www.easyeverything.com
→ *Reguliersbreestraat 22* (D C1) *Daily 9am–10pm*
→ *Damrak 33* (A C2) *Daily 9am–10pm*

ALTERNATIVE AMSTERDAM

By bicycle
For bike rentals, *see* the Transportation section at the back of this book.
Yellow Bike (A B2)
→ *Nieuwezijds Kolk 29*
Tel. 620 69 40 Price 17 €
For a guided ride around the city or an escape into the countryside. Bicycles provided.
By boat
Riverboats
→ *Cruise lasts approx. 1 hr*

Price 8.50 €
Departure points along the Prins Hendrikkade (opposite Centraal Station), from the Damrak, the Rokin or near the Stadhouderskade (behind the Rijksmuseum).
Canal Bus
→ *Weteringschans 24*
Tel. 626 55 74
Daily 9.50am–6pm
Three lines, 14 stops near the main sights. The day ticket (16 €) includes reductions on admission price for some museums.
Rederij Lovers
→ *Prins Henrikkade 25–27*
Tel. 530 10 90
◆ Museumboots line:
Seven stops. Daily 9.30am–5pm. Day pass 14.25 €
This connects the main museums. Reductions on museum admission prices.
◆ Artisexpress line:
Daily 10am–6pm
Day pass 19 €
Connects the station and

the Artis Park. Discounts for entry to the zoo, and the Tropical and Maritime History museums.
Pedalos (CanalBike) (C C4)
→ *Keisegrecht/Leidestraat, Rijksmuseum, Leidseplein, Anne Frankhuis*
Tel. 626 55 74 Daily 10am–6pm (9.30pm in summer).
7 € person/hr.
Water-taxis (A C2)
→ *From the landing piers*
Tel. 535 63 63
1–8 persons: min. 80 € for the first 30 mins, then 65 € for every additional 30 mins (+ 7 € for tel. reservations). Drinks and snacks on board.
By foot
One of the best ways to appreciate the city (itineraries available from the tourist office).
Mee in Mokum (C C2)
→ *Keisergracht 346*
Tel. 625 13 90
Mon-Fri 1–4pm. Visits:
Tue-Sun from 11am; 3 €
Pensioners proud of their

Welcome to Amsterdam!

A Centraal Station / Nieuwmarkt / Dam / Spui
B Western islands / Jordaan / Northern canals
C Southern canals / Singel / Leidseplein

D Southern canals / Rembrandtplein / Amstel
E Vondelpark / Museumplein / De Pijp
F Waterlooplein / Plantage / Oosterdok

TRANSFORMATORWEG
TASMANSTRAAT
WESTERPARK
WESTERPARK
HOUTMANKADE
HAARLEMMERWEG
HAARLEMMERWEG
BEGRAAF-
PLAATS
VREDENHOF
KADE
1e
MARNIX-
PLANTSOEN
NASSAU-
JORDAAN
Marnix-
plein
ANNE FRANK
HUIS
ERASMUSPARK
JAN VAN GALENSTRAAT
WESTERKERK
RAADHUIS-
STR.
ROZENGRACHT
B
OUDE
STAD
DE CLERQSTRAAT
BIJBELS
MUSEUM
NASSAUKADE
OUDE WEST
A
OVERTOOM
STADHOUDERSKADE
RIJKSMUSEUM
C
OVERTOOM
VONDELPARK
VAN GOGH
MUSEUM
D
Museum-
plein
ZUID
AMSTELVEENSEWEG
DE LAIRESSESTRAAT
CORNELIS KRUSEMANSTRAAT
HOBBEMAKADE
DE
Olympia-
plein
STADIONWEG
E

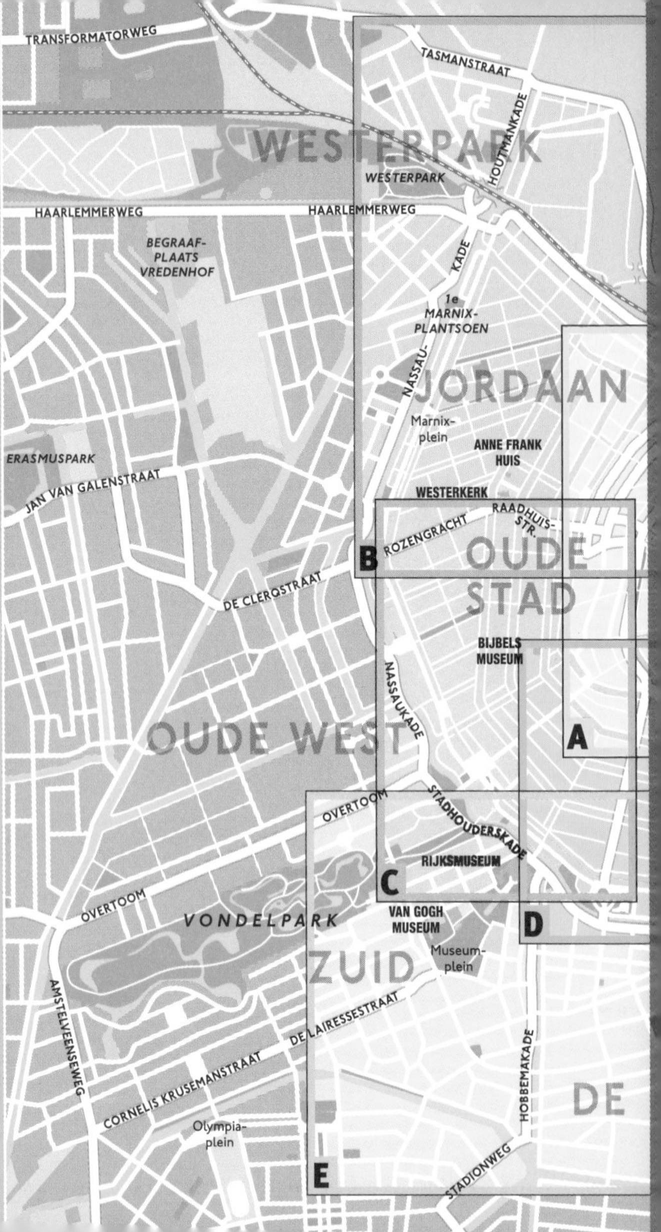

The center of Amsterdam revolves around three main squares. The historic heart, the Dam, from which the city derives its name, is surrounded by symbols of commercial glory (the Royal Palace, the Nieuwe Kerk and, further afield, the Stock Exchange). To the east, the Nieuwmarkt sports its dollhouse façades and the huge Waal (public weighing house) is unscathed by the passing of time. To the south, the Spui, the university neighborhood, draws intellectuals to its cafés, book market and to the splendid Art Nouveau Athenaeum bookstore. To the north of these squares lies the official prostitution area: the Red Light District, a maze of alley-ways and crooked houses.

UPSTAIRS

RESTAURANTS

Upstairs (**A** B5)
→ *Grimburgwal 2*
Tel. 626 56 03
Thu-Mon noon–6pm
(5.30pm Sat; 5pm Sun)
The smallest restaurant in Europe (20 square yards!), on the upper story of a narrow building, only accommodates four tables. Sweet or savory pancakes are on offer.

Café Bern (**A** D4)
→ *Nieuwmarkt 9*
Tel. 622 00 34 Daily 4pm–1am (service 6–11pm).
Closed five weeks July-Aug
Highly prized for its cheese fondues. The ideal accompaniment is a steak, grilled at the table. Reservations essential. Fondue 14 €.
À la carte 15–25 €.

Kapitein Zeppo's (**A** B5)
→ *Gebed Zonder End 5*
Tel. 624 20 57
Daily 11am–3.30pm,
5.30–11pm. Café: Sun-Thu 11am–1am (3am Fri-Sat)
This quiet restaurant, tucked away at the end of an unassuming alley, is mainly patronized by students and lecturers from the nearby university. Inventive, varied cooking (fried mussels, sea bass with langoustines, guinea-fowl with onion compote).

Live music on Thursday evenings in winter. Sit under the glass roof or the terrace. Reservation advisable. À la carte 25

Kantjil en de Tijger (**A**
→ *Spuistraat 291–293*
Tel. 620 09 94
Daily 4.30pm–11pm
At first sight, the Kantjil hardly enticing, but it of some of the city's best Indonesian cooking – h portions at very reasona prices. Try the *nasi rame* a combination of five Indonesian dishes (a simplified version of the gargantuan *rijsttafe*
À la carte 17 €.

Vermeer (**A** C2)
→ *Prins Hendrikkade 59–*
Tel. 556 48 85
Mon-Sat noon–3pm, 6–1
(closed Sat lunch)
Amsterdam's Michelin-starred star is housed in 17th-century building. C dining room, impeccabl service and a gourmet menu: sea bass with a shellfish and parsley risotto, warm apricot br and butter pudding, no ice. Reservations advise
À la carte 60 €.

CAFÉS, COFFEESHC

De Jaren (**A** B5)
→ *Nieuwe Doelenstraat 2*
Tel. 625 57 71 Daily

TEMPLE HE HWA

CENTRAAL STATION

A

MUSEUM AMSTELKRING

BEURS VAN BERLAGE

★ **Centraal Station** (A C1)
Set on three artificial islands, the weighty neo-Renaissance building of Pierre Cuypers (1889) resolutely turns its back on the sea. Its construction was controversial, as its long 985-foot façade deprived the city of its historic opening onto the IJ – and marched Amsterdam into the industrial age.

★ **Schreierstoren** (A D2)
→ *Prins Hendrikkade 94*
The tower of the Weeping Women (1480), the remains of a medieval rampart, owes its name to the women who used this vantage point to watch the sailors departing onboard Dutch vessels. It was here that Captain Henry Hudson weighed anchor in 1609 in search of a western route to the East Indies. He would later disembark in New York.

★ **Temple He Hwa** (A C3)
→ *Zeedijk 106–118*
Tel. 420 23 57 Daily noon–5pm. Closed Jan 1
An unexpected pagoda, on the city's main Chinese street. Europe's first Chinese Buddhist temple (of the Taiwanese Fo Guang Shan order) was opened on September 15, 2000 in the presence of Queen Beatrix.

★ **Oude Kerk** (A C3)
→ *Oudekerksplein 23*
Tel. 625 82 84
www.oudekerk.nl
Mon–Sat 11am–5pm; Sun 1–5pm. Closed Jan 1, April 30, Dec 25
The red neons of the prostitutes' windows shine onto Amsterdam's oldest church (early 14th century). Inside, only the three stained-glass windows in the Virgin's Chapel (1555) have survived the iconoclastic fury that swept through the city in 1556. The tower has 47 bells.

★ **Museum Amstelkring** (A C3)
→ *Oudezijds Voorburgwal 40*
Tel. 624 66 04
Mon–Sat 10am–5pm; Sun and public hols 1–5pm. Closed Jan 1, April 30
After the Netherlands' adherence to the Reformation (1578), the Church's goods were confiscated and freedom of worship abolished. Bearing witness to this period is the incredible clandestine 'Good-God-in-the-loft' chapel (1663), tucked under the rafters of a bourgeois house. The rest of the museum displays a smart 17th-century interior.

★ **Beurs van Berlage** (A B3)
→ *Damrak 243*
Museum: Tel. 624 01 41. Tue–Sun 11am–5pm

STOLOTTI HUIS

KSMUSEUM

RED LIGHT DISTRICT

Area authorized for prostitution, bounded by Damstraat, Kloverniers-burgwal, Zeedijk and Warmoestraat (**A** C3). It owes its name to the red neon signs in the prostitutes' windows. Their activity is unionized and subject to taxation.

GAY AMSTERDAM

Amsterdam is Europe's principal gay city.
Information website
→ www.gayamsterdam.com
Pink Point
→ Westermarkt (**B** B6)
noon–6pm
www.pinkpoint.org

DRUGS

Consuming, growing and dealing are illegal, but there is a distinction between soft drugs (decriminalized under 5 grams/0.17oz) and hard (penalized) drugs. Never buy anything in the street.
Coffeeshops
These cafés are intended to protect cannabis users from hard-drugs dealers. Herb is sold in sachets or as joints and smoked on the premises; prices vary according to quality.
Hash Marihuana Museum (A C4)
Oud. Achterburgwal 148
Tel. 623 59 61

xury boutiques
ng P. C. Hoofstraat and
Baerlestraat (**E** B1).
ng ready-to-wear
best shopping streets
Kalverstraat,
uwendijk (**A** B3-4),
rlemmerstraat and
rlemmerdijk (**B** C3-4).
usual shops
he 9 stratjes shopping
a: nine alleys running
he big canals, from
straat to Wijde Heisteeg
31-C3).
tique dealers
und the Spiegelkwartier:
egelstraat, Nieuwe
egelstraat and
egelgracht (**C** C5).
ard Kramer (**C** C5)
Nieuwe Spiegelstraat 64
623 08 32

ARKETS

neral market
ert Cuypstraat (**E** E2)
Mon-Sat 9am–5pm
biggest in the city.

Flower market
Singel (**C** D3)
→ Daily 8.30am–6pm
Amstelveld (**D** D3)
→ April-Nov
Mon 9am–5pm
Flea market
Waterlooplein (**F** B3)
→ Mon-Sat 9am–5pm
Noordermarkt (**B** C4)
→ Mon 9am–1pm
Birds and farm produce
Noordermarkt (**B** C4)
→ Sat 9am–4pm
Antiques
Nieuwmarkt (**A** C4)
→ May-Sep: Sun 9am–5pm
Elandsgracht (**C** B2)
→ nº 109
Sat-Thu 11am–5pm
Books and prints
Spui (**A** A5)
→ March-Oct: Fri 10am–6pm
Oudemanhuispoort (**A** B5)
→ Mon-Sat 1pm–6pm
Stamps and coins (**D** D3)
Nieuwezijds
Voorburgwal (**A** A5)
→ nº 280
Wed & Sat 1–4pm

RESTAURANTS

Eating habits
Breakfast is usually just a sandwich or salad in an eetcafé (brasserie) or a 'big café'. Dinner is the main meal, served 6–8pm.
Restaurants
Opening hours
Service 6–10pm (last orders). Reserve ahead.
Price
Prices always include VAT (BTW). Be warned – credit cards are rarely accepted.
Tips
It is customary to leave 5% of the total bill (or to round it up).
Snacks
Vlaams Frites Huis (**A** A5)
→ Voetboogstraat 33
Tel. 624 60 75 Daily 11–6pm
The best 'Belgian' fries in town, 20 different sauces.
Price 1.60 €.
Smoked fish
From March to December many stalls selling smoked

fish spring up along the streets of Amsterdam. Take advantage of your walks to sample the local specialty broodje haring, a sandwich made of milky bread with raw herring, onions and gherkins. From 2–3 €.

CAFÉS, COFFEESHOPS

Brown ('bruin') cafés
Traditional cafés that owe their name to their dark walls, stained by three centuries of tobacco smoke.
Big cafés
They serve salads and sandwiches at lunchtime. Trendy design, hip clientele.
Proeflokaal
Tasting bars specializing in jenever (gin-like spirit made from juniper berries), beer and liqueurs.
Coffeeshops
Coffeeshops also function as cafés, and can be visited just for a drink. See insert above: 'Drugs'.

AMSTERDAM AND ITS SURROUNDING AREA

SHOWS

Reservations
AUB Ticket-shop / Uitburo
→ *Leidseplein 26*
Tel. 621 12 11 Daily 9am–
9pm (by telephone)
Uitlijn
→ *Tel. 0900 01 91*
Daily 10am–9pm
Listings
Day by Day
Monthly VVV Magazine in
English; on sale at the VVV
and in bookstores.
Uitkrant
→ *In kiosks and Uitburo, free*
Monthly magazine in
Dutch, edited by the VVV.
The most complete events
listing in Amsterdam.

CALENDAR OF EVENTS

April
World Press Photo (until
May); **National Museum
weekend** (3rd of month):
all the museums are free;
Koninginnedag (30th):

street shows to celebrate
the Queen's birthday.
May
Liberation Day (5th):
popular festival, street
performances;
Drum Rhythm Festival.
June-July
Amsterdam Art Adventure
(until Aug): very varied
cultural festival;
Festival on the Ij (all
summer): dance, theater,
music in the NDMS
shipyards; **open-air
theater** in the Vondelpark
Openluchttheater;
Holland Festival:
the country's biggest
cultural event.
August
Uitmark (last weekend):
opening of cultural season
with open-air shows;
Gay Pride (first weekend):
floating stage opposite
the Pulitzer Hotel.
September
Bloemencorso (first Sat):
parade of flower-decked

floats from Aalsmeer to
Dam; **Monumentendag**
(second Sat): access to
listed buildings and
monuments;
Jordaan Festival (ten days,
second week).
November
Cannabis Cup (third week):
prize for the best herb,
the best coffeeshop, etc.
December
**Amsterdam Winter
Adventure** (until March):
thematic exhibitions
in the museums.

VIEWS OF THE CITY

Westerkerk (**B** B6)
→ *Summer:*
Mon-Fri 11am–5pm
Views from the tower.
Oude Kerk (**A** C3)
→ *Visits Wed-Sat 2–4pm*
Vista of the city's rooftops.
Beurs van Berlage (**A** B3)
View with commentary.
NeMo (**F** C1)
The Ij from atop the *Plazza*

GETTING AWAY

By train, bus or bicycle
(1–2 days). Routes on
offer at the VVV.
Waterland
Beautiful region, with
farmland, dykes and
irrigation channels,
nature reserve
Marken/Volendam/Edam
Some 15 miles from
Amsterdam, three
villages, easily accessible
by bus or bicycle. See
locals in traditional
costumes. Volendam
can be reached by boat
from Marken.
Cheese market
→ *Edam: July-Aug*
Wed 9am–2pm
Zaanse Schans
→ *7½ miles from*
Amsterdam
Windmills, clog factory,
cheese dairy... Free tours.
Flower region
Fields of tulips, narcissi,
hyacinths, from Haarlem
to Leiden. Bicycle route:
bicycle rental at Haarlem
station, return bikes to
Leiden station.
Keukenhof
→ *Late March-May*
Tel. (025) 246 55 55
The biggest floral park
in the world (70 acres).
Between Hillegom and
Lisse.
Gooï
Bicycle lane along
the Vecht river.
Muiden-Naarden
Stop to see the fortified
city of Naarden (15 miles).
Muiden Castle
→ *Tel. (0294) 26 13 25*
Aalsmeer
Flower exchange
→ *Tel. (0297) 39 21 85*
Largest flower auction
market in the world.
Mon–Sat from 7.30am.

CONSCIOUS DREAMS KOKOPELLI

OUTLAND RECORDS

10am–1am (2am Fri-Sat)
Unquestionably the most beautiful of all the city's 'big cafés', located in a former bank building. Sit and read over a coffee, or while away the time on one of the two terraces overlooking the Amstel. Delicious sandwiches and salads.

De Drie Fleschjes (**A** B3)
→ *Gravenstraat 18*
Tel. 624 84 43 Mon-Sat 1–8.30pm; Sun 3–7pm
An old *proeflokaal*, oblivious to the passing of time since 1650. You drink standing up, in a thick cloud of smoke, between the counter and a row of old barrels replete with gin, brandy, liqueurs, beers and a variety of wines.

Barney's (**A** B1)
→ *Haarlemmerstraat 102*
Tel. 625 97 61
Daily 7am–8pm
Aside from its selection of cannabis, this coffeeshop offers very good breakfasts, served throughout the day.

Café Cuba (**A** D4)
→ *Nieuwmarkt 3*
Tel. 627 49 19 Daily noon–1am (3am Fri-Sat)
Havana oozes from the rundown walls of this wonderful café. Yellowing chandeliers with glass beads, peeling paint, old

posters – everything is deliberately ramshackle. In summer it spreads onto a terrace the south side of the Nieuwmarkt, the site of the old public weighing house.

BARS, THEATER, MUSIC VENUES

De Engelenbak (**A** B4)
→ *Nes 71 Tel. 626 68 66*
www.engelenbak.nl
Evening performance 8.30pm; matinée 2.30pm
This theater is a major showcase for amateur theater, and a breeding ground for many professional groups. Musical comedies, mime, opera, cabaret. The open nights ('Open Bak') on Tuesdays attract large, eclectic crowds.

Bar Bep (**A** A4)
→ *Nieuwezijds Voorburgwal 260*
Tel. 626 56 49 Mon-Fri 5pm–1am (3am Fri); Sat-Sun 4pm–1am (3am Sat)
Bar Bep is the haunt of fashionable photographers and movie directors, and is an especially hip place to hang out in the evenings. It is an ideal introduction to Amsterdam's nightlife.

De Buurvrouw (**A** B4)
→ *Sint Pieterspoortsteeg*

29 Tel. 625 96 54 Sun-Thu 9pm–3am (4am Fri-Sat)
The favorite spot for inveterate nightowls after other clubs have closed for the night. Here, dancing goes on late and, to top it all, there is no admission charge.

In't Aepjen (**A** C2)
→ *Zeedijk 1*
Tel. 626 84 01 Daily 3pm–1am (3am Fri-Sat)
This tiny café situated close to the port has all the atmosphere of an old dockside bar. On Saturday evenings you can listen to sea shanties from the mists of time, accompanied by an accordion.

SHOPPING

Conscious Dreams Kokopelli (**A** C2)
→ *Warmoesstraat 12*
Tel. 421 70 00
www.consciousdreams.nl
Daily 11am–10pm
The second Conscious Dreams outlet to open in Amsterdam, it is a gallery-cum-store, and sells cacti, books and vitamins, but also herbal ecstasies, Guarana capsules, joints and magic mushrooms... The shop assistants are expert on the subject and full of good advice.

Geel's en Co (**A** C3)
→ *Warmoesstraat 67*
Tel. 624 06 83 www.geels.nl
Mon-Sat 9.30am–6pm
Museum: Sat 2–5pm
Traditional tea and coffee shop founded over 140 years ago. The coffee, ground on the spot, gives off this unique, all-embracing aroma. Samples on request.

Jacob Hooy & Co (**A** C4)
→ *Kloveniersburgwal 12*
Tel. 624 30 41 Mon-Sat 10am–6pm (5pm Sat)
www.jacobhooy.nl
Ever since 1743, the walls of this antiquated herbalist's shop have been impregnated with the smells of the Orient. Old casks and drawers stuffed with medicinal herbs, teas, a host of spices and cosmetic or therapeutic oils pack every inch of space. Also available, homeopathic medicine and delicious aromatic herb candies.

Outland Records (**A** C2)
→ *Zeedijk 22 Tel. 638 75 76*
Mon 1–6pm; Tue-Sat 11am–6pm (9pm Thu)
Techno, trance, jungle, drum 'n' bass, hard house; a wide range of CDs and vinyl records for beginner and expert DJs alike. Free use of decks for listening or scratching.

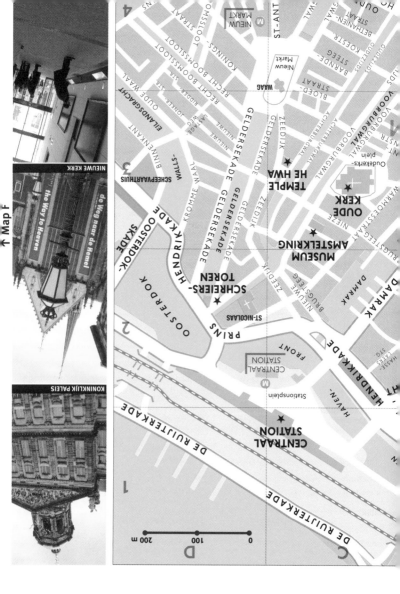

BEGIJNHOF

ALLARD PIERSON MUSEUM

out question the
t important work by
 Berlage (1903). The
itect's functional lines
is brick, glass and
l building forged key
cepts that would mark
vork and, by ushering
odern architecture,
enced all of Europe.
 a cultural center, it
ains a museum of the
ding's history.

**oninklijk
is (A** A3)
am   Tel. 620 40 60
-July: Mon-Fri 11am–5pm;
guided tour Wed 2pm.
sionally open in Sep-June
y of the great artists of
period worked on the

Town Hall (1665), designed
in the purist Dutch classical
style by Jacob van Campen.
Both inside and out, reliefs,
friezes, flagstones and
caryatids recall the city's
naval supremacy. Louis
Bonaparte turned it into a
royal palace in 1808.
Today's queen rarely stays.

★ **Amsterdams
Historisch Museum /
Schuttersgalerij (A** A4)
→ Nieuwezijds Voorburgwal
357 Tel. 523 18 22
www.ahm.nl
Mon-Fri 10am– 5pm;
Sat-Sun 11am–5pm.
Closed Jan 1, April 30, Dec 25
All the city's history: its
expansion, its outstanding

figures, its daily life, from
the 13th century to the
present day. In the Civil
guard gallery, portraits of
the bourgeois militias
responsible for defending
the city in the 17th century.

★ **Nieuwe Kerk (A** A3)
→ Dam   Tel. 638 69 09
Daily 10am–6pm (9pm Thu)
A basilica with elaborate
late Gothic transept (early
15th century), partly hidden
by the adjoining Royal
Palace. Dutch sovereigns
were once crowned here.

★ **Begijnhof (A** A5)
→ Spui, between nos 37 & 38
Mon 1–6.30pm; Tue-Sun
9am–6.30pm (6pm Sat-Sun)
A sleepy courtyard flanked

by 17th- and 18th-century
houses, once a Beguine
convent (1665). Do not
miss the city's oldest
house (1477), the church
(15th century) and
clandestine chapel (1665)
spread around the garden.

★ **Allard Pierson
Museum (A** B5)
→ Oude Turfmarkt 127
Tel. 525 25 56
Tue-Fri 10am–5pm;
Sat-Sun & public hols 1–5pm.
Closed Jan 1, April 30, Easter
and Whit sundays
University museum
dedicated to everyday life
in ancient times. Incredible
collections. Recommended
to archeology enthusiasts.

WEST INDISCH HUIS

NOORDERKERK

★ West Indisch Huis (B D4)
→ *Haarlemmerstraat 75*
The West India Company (1621–1791) was not as prestigious as its older sibling, the East India Company. Its profits were mainly derived from the slave trade and piracy. One of its more daring exploits is still etched in the memory: the attack on the Spanish silver fleet (1628). The fabulous booty was stored in the cellars of this building. In the courtyard, a statue of Peter Stuyvesant, the Governor of New Holland (1647–64), and a stele mural depicting the birth of the Dutch colony in America.

★ Brouwersgracht (B C4)
Named the brewers' canal in the 17th century because of its main local activity, the brewing of beer. For a long time this was a dark and smelly industrial zone. Spices, sugar, coffee, whale oil and other goods from distant lands were once piled up in the ware-houses along the quays. They were hoisted up by pulleys on the roofs and passed through the large vaulted windows. Today, Brouwersgracht is a lively area, prized for its houseboats and its ware-houses converted into lofts.

★ Noorderkerk (B C4)
→ *Noordermarkt*
Hendrick de Keyser's church (1623), built for the Jordaan workers, inspired a host of other Protestant churches. The architect drew on Catholic tradition by building around a Greek cross, which made the pulpit a focal point. Every week in the square are held a flea market (Monday), and a bird and poultry market (Saturday 9am–4pm).

★ Prinseneiland (B C3)
On the edge of the city, the Prince's Island seems stuck in time. Sailboats bob sleepily on the water, while the open doors of warehouses wait in vain cargo. Linked to the oth islands by delicate mob bridges, the old extensi the seaport has eluded wrecking ball. Its indust buildings, bought up by artists, now contain bot public housing and sumptuous lofts.

★ Sint Andrieshofje (B A5)
→ *Egelantiersgracht 107*
The city's second-oldes *hofje* (1616), after the Beguine convent. The entrance corridor decorated with Delft tile leads onto a peaceful courtyard planted with

PRINSENEILAND

Map labels:

AUKADE

NIXSTRAAT

LIJNBAANSGRACHT

MARNIXSTRAAT

FAGELSTRAAT

ANTONIE HEINSIUSSTRAAT

JACOB CATSKADE

JACOB CATSKADE

KATTESLOOT

DE WITTENSTRAAT

KOSTVERLORENVAART

VAN BEUNINGENSTRAAT

GOUDSBLOEM

WILLEMSSTR.

PALM-DWARSSTR.

PALMGRACHT

BAANGRACHT

BROUWERS GRACHT

NIEUWE WILLEMSSTRAAT

MARNIXKADE

SINGELGRACHT

NASSAUKADE

1e MARNIX-PLANTSOEN

DE WITTENKADE

NASSAUSTRAAT

WITTENSTRAAT

DE KOSTVERLORENKADE

VAN HOGENDORPSTRAAT

DE WITTENKADE

F.SCHOTENSTR.

Haarlemmer-plein

Nassau-plein

STRAAT

VAN LIMBURG

WESTER-PARK

HAARLEMMERWEG

HAARLEMMERVAART

WESTERPARK

WESTERPARK

2

HOUTMANSTR.

WESTERKANAAL

HOUTMANSTRAAT

WESTZAANSTR.

WESTZAANSTRAAT

ZAANSTRAAT

ZAANDIJK STRAAT

ZAANSTRAAT

VAN NOORDTKADE

VAN NOORDT-GRACHT

LE MAIRE GRACHT

Suiker-plein

POLANENSTRAAT

POLANENSTR.

WORMERVEERSTR.

SPAARNDAMMERSTRAAT

SPAARNDAMMER PLANTSOEN

KNOLLENDAMSTR.

NOVA ZEMBLASTRAAT

HOUTRIJKSTRAAT

HEMBRUGSTRAAT

OOSTZAANSTRAAT

TASMANSTRAAT

TASMANSTRAAT

GEVLEWEG

STAANGERWEG

GEVLEWEG

Zaandammer-plein

1

A

B

C

4

From its popular past Jordaan has retained its modest houses with their flower-bedecked windows and an intense neighborhood spirit. Convivial cafés, where alcohol flows freely and incongruous shops lurk round the corners of its shady streets. This *joie de vivre* has taken over the big canals: restaurants and brightly colored shopfronts throng the maze of alleyways along their banks. To the north, Haarlemmerdijk buzzes with coffeeshops and cheap hotels. Beyond the railway line, three interconnected islands, with their old warehouses and disused docks, are a memorial to the city's maritime history.

DE BOLHOED

DE BELHAMEL

RESTAURANTS

Balraj (**B** C3)
→ *Haarlemmerdijk 28*
Tel. 625 14 28
Daily 4.30–10.30pm
Excellent northern Indian cooking at very low prices. All the dishes (chicken in yogurt and coconut milk, curried lamb) are accompanied by fried rice, *chapati* and lentils. Vegetarian dishes.
À la carte 13 €.

De Bolhoed (**B** C5)
→ *Prinsengracht 60–62*
Tel. 626 18 03
Daily noon–10pm
For devotees of vegetarian cuisine and organic food. By day: soups, quiches and hot or cold sandwiches (hummus, *tahini*, feta). At night: vegetables (spinach, mushrooms, broccoli, corn), brown rice and salad. Homemade pies and cakes. À la carte 20 €.

Griet Manshande (**B** C3)
→ *Keerpunt 10*
Tel. 622 81 94
Wed-Sun 6–10pm
A local favorite, nestling on the Bickereiland. Provençal imaginative cuisine prepared by the chef in full view of the customers. Pretty shaded terrace. Set menu 21 €.

Vijf (**B** C5)
→ *Prinsenstraat 10*
Tel. 428 24 55
www.restaurantzest.nl
Tue-Sun 6pm–midnight
Lunch by arrangement for groups
A mix of Mediterranean and Oriental cooking in a stylish, sober, black and cream decor. 'Semi-vegetarian' dishes such as tabouleh and sushi. Eclectic wine list.
À la carte 35 €.

De Belhamel (**B** D4)
→ *Brouwersgracht 60*
Tel. 622 10 95
www.belhamel.nl Daily 6–10pm (10.30pm Fri-Sat)
The gold and brown Art Deco interior alone deserves a visit. Further reasons are the excellent French-Italian cuisine and the stunning views over Brouwersgracht and Herengracht. A favorite with Amsterdammers.
Set menu 32 €.
À la carte 40 €.

CAFÉS, COFFEESHOP

Villa ZeeZicht (**B** C6)
→ *Torensteeg 7*
Tel. 626 74 33
Daily 7.30am–10pm (8pm Sun)
Café situated on the banks of the Singel. Good breakfasts (yogurts,

ZO

THE PURPLE ONION

SANTA JET

fruit juices, milkshakes) and sandwiches, but it is the homemade cakes that have made the café's reputation.

De Reiger (B B5)
→ Nieuwe Leliestraat 34
Tel. 624 74 26 Daily
11am–1am (2am Fri-Sat)
The most modern of the city's old bistros, where one drinks a glass of good wine by the candlelight flickering on the heavy, red velvet drapes. Packed at mealtimes.

Café Tabac (B C4)
→ Brouwersgracht 101
Tel. 622 44 13 Tue-Fri
4pm–1am (3am Fri); Sat-Mon 11am–1am (3am Sat)
Laid-back setting and young clientele. Dim sum and excellent bagel sandwiches. Opposite is the tiny brown café Het Papeneiland, dating from 1641.

Siberië (B D4)
→ Brouwersgracht 11
Tel. 623 59 09
www.siberie.nl
Daily 11am–11pm
(midnight Fri-Sat)
Coffeeshop with small-scale cultural program (exhibitions, live jazz, poetry, 'open mike' evenings, DJs) seen through clouds of Siberian Tiger or Amsterdam Delight (Dutch hash).

BARS, CLUBS, MOVIE THEATER

Westergasfabriek (B A2)
→ Haarlemmerweg 8–10
Tel. 586 07 10
www.westergasfabriek.nl
An old gas factory converted into a huge cultural complex: with a theatre, movie theaters, festivals, exhibitions. See also the arthouse movie theater Het Ketelhuis (www.ketelhuis.nl).

The Movies (B B3)
→ Haarlemmerdijk 161
Tel. 638 60 16
www.themovies.nl
Lovely early 20th-century movie theater, attractive for both its Art Deco interior and its program. The public provides spontaneous movie criticism in the café-restaurant.

Mazzo (B A6)
→ Rozengracht 114
Tel. 626 75 00
www.mazzo.nl Thu-Sun
11pm–4am (5am Fri-Sat)
Small in size but big in crowds. Deep house, funk, groovy house.

Cafe'Nol (B B4)
→ Westerstraat 109
Tel. 624 53 80 Wed-Mon
9pm–3am (4am Fri-Sat)
All the spirit of Jordaan's most popular traditions:

old-fashioned decor, romantic songs, accordion playing, and even karaoke nights. Mixed clientele, both old and young, who appreciate the genuine kitsch of the place.

SHOPPING

House of Tattoos (B C3)
→ Haarlemmerdijk 130c
Tel. 330 90 46
www.houseoftattoos.nl
Mon-Sat 11am–6pm
Sjab Horwitz helps his customers create their own design. Tattoos after consultation, for over-18s only, by appointment.

The Purple Onion (B C3)
→ Haarlemmerdijk 139
Tel. 427 37 50 Tue-Sat
11.30am–6pm (5pm Sat)
Indian fabrics with hand-sewn gold embroidery, silver-plated chairs with purple velvet upholstery to turn a home into a palace straight out of The Arabian Nights.

Meeuwig & Zn (B D4)
→ Haarlemmerstraat 70
Tel. 626 52 86
Mon-Fri 11am–6.30pm;
Sat 10am–5.30pm
A Mediterranean deli in Amsterdam. All the ingredients for vinaigrette sauces: raspberry and apple vinegars, mustards

with honey, oil from Tuscany, etc.

Hempworks (B D4)
→ Niewendijk 13
Tel. 421 17 62 Daily
11am–7pm (9pm Thu-Sat)
A store that specializes in hemp products, including a line of clothing and cosmetics. The owner can also give advice on the best coffeeshops of the moment.

Brilmuseum Brillenwinkel (B C6)
→ Gasthuismolensteeg 7
Tel. 421 24 14 www.
brilmuseumamsterdam.nl
Wed-Fri 11.30am–5.30pm;
Sat noon–5pm
A small spectacle museum-cum-store with hundreds of different types of spectacles, dating from the 19th century to the present day. Online shop.

Santa Jet (B C5)
→ Prinsenstraat 7
Tel. 427 20 70
Mon-Fri 11am–6pm;
Sat-Sun 10am–5pm
(noon Sun)
A temple of kitsch religious imagery from Mexico. Posters of saints, Madonna shampoo bottles, decorated candles, but also colored-glass lamps, floral plastic aprons, Mexican comics and much more.

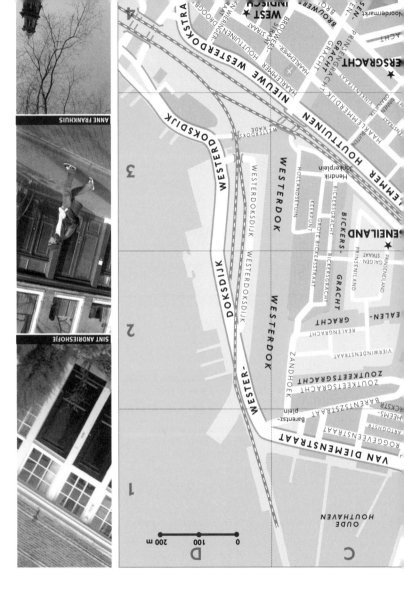

ANNE FRANKHUIS

SINT ANDRIESHOFJE

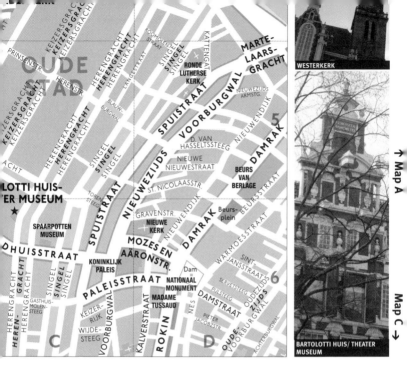

WESTERKERK

BARTOLOTTI HUIS/ THEATER MUSEUM

→ Map A

Map C →

ers and bordered by
l houses, formerly
rved for destitute
rly people.

nne Frankhuis (B B5)
→ *rinsengracht 263*
56 71 00
March: daily 9am–5pm
*1 April-Aug). Jan 1: noon–
Dec 25 noon–5pm.
ed for Yom Kippur*
 year, more than
 ooo visitors squeeze
 the famous *achterhuis*
 house') where Anne
 her family were
 ned for two years,
 re being reported to
 Gestapo and deported
 44. The front of the
 e is now a museum

commemorating the Shoah.
Long queues in summer:
arrive well before it opens.
★ **Westerkerk (B** B6)
→ *Prinsengracht 281*
Tel. 624 77 66
*April-Sep: Mon-Fri 11am–3pm
(July-Aug: Sat 11am–3pm)*
First Protestant church
built after the Reformation
(1620), the work of Hendrick
de Keyser. Its 280-foot bell
tower stands over the entire
city, proudly displaying one
of the symbols of
Amsterdam: the Imperial
crown that Maximilian of
Austria added to the city's
coat of arms. A simple
façade, spare, elegant lines,
a bare interior with no altar.

The 'West Church'
introduced an aesthetic
proper to Protestantism.
★ **Bartolotti Huis /
Theater Museum (B** C6)
→ *Herengracht 168*
Tel. 551 33 00
*Tue-Fri 11am– 5pm; Sat-Sun
1–5pm. Closed Jan 1, April 30,
Dec 25*
Of the five buildings that
make up the Theater
Museum, the Bartolotti
House (n°s 170–72) is the
most exuberant. A mix of
red bricks and white stones,
indented gables adorned
with pillars, volutes and
obelisks: none of the
elements typical of the
Dutch Renaissance are

spared on the façade,
adding up to a fine example
of Hendrick de Keyser's
domestic architecture.
On the gables, the mottos
'Through capability and
hard work' and 'Religion
and rectitude' convey the
Calvinist values of the
contemporary bourgeoisie.
Inside, lush stucco
decorations, frescos and
painted ceilings are the
stage for a collection of
costumes, documents
and audio-visual archives
related to the Dutch theater.
Entrance in the sandstone
building by the great
architect Philips Vingboons
(1638).

BIJBELS MUSEUM

BLOEMENMARKT

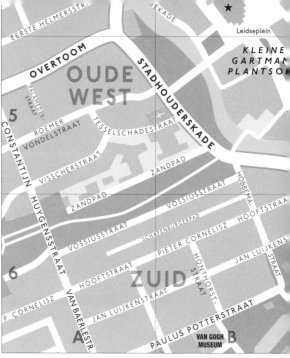

OVERTOOM

OUDE WEST

STADHOUDERSKADE

Leidseplein

KLEINE GARTMAN PLANTSO

EERSTE HELMERSSTR.

PACHMEDES-STRAAT

ROEMER VONDELSTRAAT

TESSELSCHADESTRAAT

CONSTANTIJN HUYGENSSTRAAT

VISSCHERSTRAAT

ZANDPAD

ZANDPAD

VOSSIUSSTRAAT

HOBBEMA-

VOSSIUSSTRAAT

SCHAPENBURGERPAD

PIETER CORNELISZ

HOOFTSTRAAT

HONTHORST-STRAAT

JAN LUIJKENS STRAAT

ZUID

HOOFTSTRAAT

P. CORNELISZ

VAN BAERLESTR.

JAN LUIJKENSTRAAT

PAULUS POTTERSTRAAT

VAN GOGH MUSEUM

★ **Woonbootmuseum Hendrika Maria** (**C** B2)
→ *Prinsengracht, opposite n° 296*
Tel. 427 07 50
March-Oct: Tue-Sun 11am–5pm; Nov-Feb: Fri-Sun 11am–5pm (same Easter and Whit mondays).
Closed Jan 1, April 30, Dec 25
Amsterdam's 2,500 house-boats, whether floating gardens, improvized rafts or luxurious barges, are all a treat for the eyes. They appeared as a result of the 1950s housing crisis, when they were still illegal. They are mostly moored on the Prinsengracht and the Amstel, and the museum-

boats illustrate practical aspects of life on the water (models, photos). Small display, but fun.
★ **Felix Meritis Huis** (**C** B2)
→ *Keizersgracht 324*
Tel. 623 13 11
Access to bar: Mon-Fri 9am–7pm; temporary exhibitions
In such an architecturally homogeneous city, the pomp of this neoclassical palace (1788) stands out: four robust Corinthian pillars support its sculpted pediment. The building served as the HQ of the cultural and scientific Felix Meritis Foundation ('happy by merit').

Under the influence of the Lumière brothers, it turned to teaching art and science with a view to social progress. Today, it is an experimental theater and mounts collaborations between European artists.
★ **Bijbels Museum** (**C** C3)
→ *Herengracht 366–368*
Tel. 624 24 36
www.bijbelsmuseum.nl
Mon-Sat 10am–5pm; Sun and bank hols 11am–5pm.
Closed Jan 1, April 30, Dec 25
Archeological exhibits from Egypt and the Middle East, models, manuscripts and several editions of the Bible, including one from 1477. The museum is

spread over four identic gabled houses built by Philips Vingboons, with ceilings painted by Jaco de Wit (1695–1754).
★ **Gouden Bocht** (**C** D
→ *Herengracht, betweer Leidsestrat and Vijzelstro*
It was on the shores of the Canal of the Lords, particularly along the bank known as the Gol Curve, that the richest trading and banking families of the 17th cen set up home. As a sign of their wealth, their extraordinarily opulent residences spanned four or five plots (at tha time they were not

FELIX MERITIS HUIS

WOONBOOTMUSEUM HENDRIKA MARIA

Map

4
3
2
1

A
B

WOONBOOT-MUSEUM ★

DERDE HELMERSSTR.
BOSBOOM TOUSSAINTSTR.
SINGELGRAC
LEIDSEKADE
NASSAUKADE
MARNIXSTR
LIJNBAANSGR
KLEINE LEIDSEDWARS
LEIDSEDWARS
PALL VAN JUS
LEID
LEIDS
MOLE
RUNS
MED
BER

RAAMSTRAAT
LEIDSEGRACHT
Raamplein
NIEUWE PASSEERDERS-STRAAT
PASSEERDERSGRACHT
PRINSENGRACHT
LOOIERSGRACHT
LIJNBAANSGRACHT
MARNIXSTRAAT
OUDE LOOIERSSTR.
1e LOOIERSDWARSSTR.

ELANDSGRACHT
ELANDSSTRAAT
HAZENSTRAAT
LAURIERGRACHT
1e LAURIERDWARSSTR
2e LAURIER-DWARSSTR.
LAURIERSTRAAT
LIJNBAANSGRACHT
LIJNBAANSTRAAT

ROZENSTRAAT
1e ROZEN-DWARSSTR.
2e ROZEN-DWARSSTR.
ROZENGRACHT
INST. V. TECHNICH
MARNIXSTRAAT

1e BLOEM-DWARSSTR.
2e BLOEM-DWARSSTR.
BLOEMSTRAAT
BLOEMGRACHT

The majestic canals 'of the Lords', 'of the Emperor' and 'of the Prince' – symbols of the three power bases of the 17th century – boast the city's most elegant façades. To the south is Leidseplein, taken over from dawnbreak by a terrace café, street musicians and fire-eaters. Later, nightclubs and movie theaters keep up the pace until the early hours of the morning. The Leidsestraat and the shopping area known as *9 stratjes* (the 9 streets) (from Reestraat to Wijde Heisteeg) are packed with trendy shops. To the east, the antique dealers have settled in all along the Nieuwe Spiegelstraat.

GOODIES

'T BUFFET VAN ODETTE

RESTAURANTS

A la Plancha (**C** B2)
→ *1ˢᵗ Looiersdwarsstraat 15*
Tel. 420 36 33
Tue-Sun 3pm–1am
(3am Fri-Sat). Closed Aug
Authentic tapas bar serving the traditional squid, seafood, serrano ham and marinated olives. Latin eating hours are respected: the kitchen stays in operation until closing time. À la carte 15–30 €.

Goodies (**C** C3)
→ *Huidenstraat 9*
Tel. 625 61 22
Daily noon–10pm
Trendy Italian restaurant. The menu is written on a blackboard: salmon ravioli, tortellini with blue cheese and walnuts, gnocchi with sage and butter. At lunchtime, goodies include hot or cold sandwiches, fruit juices, milkshakes, warm milk with aniseed and honey. À la carte 15–25 €.

De Smoeshaan (**C** B4)
→ *Leidsekade 90*
Tel. 625 03 68 Sun-Thu 11am–1am (3am Fri-Sat)
Restaurant belonging to the Bellevue Theater so many actors come here for a snack or a drink before the shows. Light dishes for lunch, Italian and French cuisine for dinner from 5.30pm. Typical Amsterdam brown café decor. À la carte 20 €.

Garlic Queen (**C** D3)
→ *Reguliersdwarsstraat 27*
Tel. 422 64 26
www.garlicqueen.nl
Wed-Sun 6–10pm
A restaurant specializing in garlic... The 55 lbs of bulbs ordered every week even end up in unlikely desserts, although dishes without garlic are also available. Reservations essential. À la carte 35 €.

CAFÉS, DELI

Van Puffelen (**C** B2)
→ *Prinsengracht 375–377*
Tel. 624 62 70
Mon-Fri 3pm–1am (2am Fri);
Sat-Sun 11am–1am (2am Sat)
Nothing is allowed to disturb the peace of Van Puffelen's regulars: the owners even had to cancel the (too lively) live jazz on Sundays. The preferred pastimes are reading or sunbathing by the canal.

't Buffet van Odette (**C** B2)
→ *Berenstraat 4*
Tel. 423 60 34 Mon-Fri 8.30am–5.30pm; Sat 10am–5.30pm; Sun noon–5.30pm
This tiny buffet prepares excellent sandwiches, quiches and cakes with

ONIA

FIFTIES-SIXTIES

DE KAASKAMER

organic products, to take out or eat on the spot, around the counter (only three benches). Beware, the opening hours vary.

Café Cox (C B4)
→ Marnixstraat 429
Tel. 620 72 22 *Daily service 5.30–10.30pm; Bar: 5pm–1am (3am Fri-Sat)*
A mixed crowd, often from the theater world, packs into the space between the poster-covered walls for dinner or a drink in the bar.

Bagels & Beans (C C4)
→ Keizersgracht 504
Tel. 330 55 08
www.bagelsbeans.nl
Mon-Fri 9.30am–5.30pm; Sat-Sun 10am–6pm
Mouthwatering bagel sandwiches, both savory (roast vegetables, mozzarella) and sweet (banana, maple syrup, cinnamon); fresh fruit juice too. À la carte 7 €.

BARS, SHOWS

Blakes (C C2)
→ Keizersgracht 384
Tel. 530 2010
www.blakesamsterdam.com
Have a drink at the bar of the prestigious Blakes Hotel, or even dinner if your budget allows the expense. The interior decoration of the 17th-

century building is stunning, with an East-meets-West theme in both food and decor, gorgeous fabrics, and a serene black and white lounge. Cocktails from 8 €.

De Zotte (C B4)
→ Raamstraat 29
Tel. 626 86 94 *Daily 4pm–1am (3am Fri-Sat). Last orders for food 9.30pm*
Off the beaten track, a small bar renowned for its large selection of Belgian beers (over 120 brands) and for its generous dishes.

Boom Chicago (C B4)
→ Leidseplein 12
Tel. 423 01 01
www.boomchicago.nl
Very popular theater where comedies are staged in English. Dinner is also served before the performances. The café is packed at nights.

Paradiso (C B5)
→ Weteringschans 6–8
Tel. 626 45 21
www.paradiso.nl
Famous concert hall situated in a disused church, which promotes both local groups and international stars alike.

Melkweg (C B4)
→ Lijnbaansgracht 234a
Tel. 531 81 81
www.melkweg.nl
A meeting point for hippies

in the 1970s, the Melkweg is now a versatile cultural center: music, dance, movies, photography, plus DJ nights, including *Cross fader* (Sat at midnight).

SHOPPING

Antonia (C C1)
→ Gasthuismolensteeg 6, 16–20 Tel. 627 24 33
www.AntoniabyYvette.nl
Tue-Sat 10am–6pm (9pm Thu); Sun noon–6pm
Antonia consists of three shoe shops given over to men's, women's and... slippers. From playful gaudiness to irreproachable coolness.

Fifties-Sixties (C C3)
→ Huidenstraat 13
Tel. 623 26 53
Tue-Sat 1–6pm (5.30pm Sat)
A clutter of ironware and household electrical goods from the 1930s to the 1970s: ashtrays, lamps, mixers. Aesthetic considerations aside, everything is in perfect working order!

De Kaaskamer (C B3)
→ Runstraat 7
Tel. 623 34 83 *Mon noon–6pm; Tue-Sat 9am–6pm (5pm Sat); Sun noon–5pm*
The best cheese shop in town. Large selection of country cheeses, Goudas, *Friese Nagel kaas* (flavored

with cloves) and *Leidse kaas* (with cumin). Sandwiches prepared on request.

The Frozen Fountain (C B3)
→ Prinsengracht 629
Tel. 622 93 75
Mon 1–6pm; Tue-Sat 10am–6pm (5pm Sat)
This large hall displays the best of contemporary design, with a variety of music playing in the background (from classical to techno). At the back, exhibitions of the work of young designers.

Art Multiples (C C4)
→ Keizersgracht 510
Tel. 624 84 19 www.artnl.nl
Mon 1–6pm; Tue-Sat 10am–6pm (7pm Thu); Sun noon–5pm
Comprehensive collection of posters and some 40,000 postcards classified by theme or artist (first editions): you'll be surprised how quickly time passes here.

Marañon (C D3)
→ Singel 488-490
Tel. 622 59 38
Daily 10am–5pm (11am Sun); Summer: 9am–6pm (10am Sun). www.maranon.net
Glistening hammocks from Central and South America. In cotton, fiber and hemp, they come in all styles and colors.

★ Map A

KATTEN KABINET

GOUDEN BOCHT

GOUDEN BOCHT
★ KATTEN KABINET

★ BLOEMENMARKT

KEIZERSGRACHT
KEIZERSGRACHT

HERENGRACHT
HERENGRACHT
REGULIERSDWARSSTRAAT

LEIDSESTRAAT

LEIDSEGRACHT

LEIDSEGRACHT

KEIZERSGR.

4

3

SINGEL

SINGEL

SINGEL

Konings-
plein

HEILIGEWEG

KALVERSTRAAT

VOLTERBOOG-
STRAAT

OUDE
LUTHERSE
KERK

SPUI

SPUI

ROKIN

ROKIN

ROKIN

ROKIN

KALVERSTRAAT

NIEUWEZIJDS

SPUISTRAAT

BEGIJNHOF

BIJBELS
MUSEUM
★

HUIDENSTRAAT

WIJDE HEISTEEG

HERENGRACHT

SINGEL
SINGEL

SINGEL

HERENGRACHT

HERENGRACHT

HERENGRACHT

WOLVENSTR.

KEIZERSGRACHT
KEIZERSGRACHT

HARTENSTR.

AMSTERDAMS
HISTORISCH
MUSEUM

VOORBURGWAL

WIJDE-
STEEG

MADAME TUSSAUD

RIJK
JONGE ROELEN-
STEEG

KEIZER-
STEEG

GASTHUIS-
MOLENSTEEG

SINGEL
SINGEL

SINGEL

SINGEL

OUDE
STAD

PALEISSTRAAT

SPUI-
STRAAT

RAADHUISSTRAAT

RAADHUISSTRAAT

MOZES EN
AARONSTR.

KONINKLIJK
PALEIS

SPAARPOTTEN
MUSEUM

BARTOLOTTI HUIS-
-THEATER MUSEUM

NIEUWE
KERK

GRAVENSTR.

1

C

SPIEGELGRACHT

STADSSCHOUWBURG

↑ Map D

...nitted by city ...lations to be more than ...eet wide). Note the ...ch influence on the ...des of n°⁵ 475, 476 and ...the latter the home of ...powerful Six dynasty ...ver two hundred years.

...loemenmarkt (C D3)
...ingel
... 9am–5pm
...rming flower market ...e Singel, between ...ngsplein and ...tplein. The barges have ...n moored here since ...e. Exuberant ...of colors and smells: ...s, bulbs, houseplants, ...enirs, wooden clogs. At ...fall, the lights on the

barges add to the charm of the spectacle.

★ **Katten Kabinet (C** D4)
→ *Herengracht 497*
Tel. 626 53 78
www.kattenkabinet.nl
Mon-Fri 10am–2pm; Sat-Sun and public hols 1–5pm.
Closed Dec 25–6 and Jan 1
The only house on the Golden Curve open to the public. After the death of his cat in 1984, John Pierpont Morgan III, the last of its occupants, turned it into a temple to the artistic depiction of felines. A succession of rooms displays statues, posters and objets d'art, with a few live specimens

dozing on sofas or playing in the garden.

★ **Spiegelgracht (C** C5)
From Lijnbaansgracht to Prinsengracht, a lovely shady canal flanked by dollhouses. The slightly sloping façades in most of the houses facilitated the hoisting of goods into the attic (the cellars being prone to flooding and so unsuitable for storage). Today these houses function as art galleries and antique shops, giving rise to the *spiegelwartier* or antique collectors' district. Further on is the Nieuwe Spiegelstraat, a more upmarket area.

★ **Stadsschouwburg (C** B4)
→ *Leidseplein 26*
Tel. 624 23 11
Destroyed three times by fire, the city theater was rebuilt for the last time in 1894 by Jan Springer and A. L. van Gendt in the Dutch neo-Renaissance style. It creates excitement in the Leidseplein on opening nights or when the Ajax football team is playing (its victories are announced from the balcony). The national opera and ballet companies moved to the Muziektheater after the opening of the Stopera (1986).

WETERINGDWARSSTRAAT
3e

NOORDERSTRAAT

EGULIERSGRACHT

SCHANS

LIJNBAANSGRACHT

NIEUWE LOOIERSSTRAAT

VIJZELGRAC

FOTKE SIMONSZSTRAAT

SINGELGRACHT

WETERINGSCHANS

LIJNBAANSGRACHT
LIJNBAANSGRACHT

WETERINGSCHANS

RIJKSMUSEUM

STADHOUDERSKADE

WETERING-
PLANTSOEN

DEN TEXSTRAAT

NICOLAAS

HOBBEMAKADE

RUYSDAELKADE

NICOLAAS WITSENKADE

SINGELGRACHT

0   100   200 m

**HEINEKEN
BROUWERIJ**

A   **B**   **C** STADH

REGULIERSGRACHT

MAGERE BRUG

★ Rembrandtplein
(**D** C2)

This square once housed the first public weighing house, *waag*, (the last one is still in existence today, in Nieuwmarkt) and a butter market. Rechristened Rembrandtplein in 1876, the center of the square is adorned by a statue of the painter, his gaze turned toward the Jewish Quarter, where he lived before his bankruptcy and subsequent move to the Jordaan district. Rembrandtplein, lined with cafés and bars, is now one of the focal points of Amstel's nightlife.

★ Tuschinskitheater
(**D** C1)

→ *Reguliersbreestraat 26–28*
Tel. 626 15 13
www.tuschinski.nl
Art Deco masterpiece or kitsch nightmare? The decorative exuberance of the eccentric Tuchinski Theater (stained glass, turrets, sculptures), built in 1921 and then converted into a movie theater, leaves no room for indifference. The craziness continues inside, with an onslaught of tapestries, lamps and paintings of extraordinary lavishness and exoticism. The carpet in the lobby, once ruined by cigarette

butts, has been completely rewoven by hand. Several screens, but n° 1 remains the most authentic.

★ Munttoren (**D** C1)
→ *Muntplein*
The Mint Tower overlooks the confluence of the Singel and the Amstel. The minting operation was transferred here in 1672–3, under the threat of an invasion by Louis XIV's troops. Its wooden super-structure (1620) was built by the greatest architect of the time, Hendrick de Keyser, to cover the Regulierspoort tower remains (1490). In the lantern, a set of bells made by the Hémony brothers.

★ Museum Willet-Holthuysen (**D** D2)
→ *Herengracht 605*
Tel. 523 18 70
Mon-Fri 10am–5pm; Sat and public hols 11am–5p
Closed Jan 1, April 30, De
Built in 1687, this beau patrician house was h to many rich Amstel families. In 1860 its las owners, a couple of collectors and art lover gave it over to the city, which turned it into a museum of Dutch inte Glassware, engravings clocks and porcelain, mainly from the 18th a 19th centuries, fill the rooms on each floor.

Map 1

Reguliersdwarsstraat and Amstelstraat, tucked away behind the river Amstel, boast the greatest number of gay nightclubs and meeting places in the city. These two streets open onto the Rembrandtplein, where other urban groups gather in the cafés and fashionable clubs. To the south, Utrechtsestraat is studded with trendy restaurants and shops. Close by, but light years away from all this hubbub, lies a Protestant wooden church, the Amstelkerk (1669), with its peaceful square where children play hopscotch opposite the shaded terrace of the Kort café.

ZUSHI TAKE THAÏ

RESTAURANTS

Tujuh Maret (D D3)
→ *Utrechtsestraat 73*
Tel. 427 98 65
Mon-Sat noon–10pm;
Sun 5–10pm
www.tujuh-maret.nl
The cuisine of Mina Hasa, in the north of the island of Sulawesi, takes root in Amsterdam. To try a little of everything, choose a combination of Indonesian dishes: *nasi rames* (five dishes), *nasi kuning Tujuh Maret* (ten dishes), *rijsttafel Mina Hasa* (18 dishes), all accompanied by rice, prawn chips and a salad of choice. The flavors range from sweet to spicy or very spicy indeed. À la carte 18–20 €.

Vooges (D D2)
→ *Utrechtsestraat 51*
Tel. 330 56 70
Daily 6–11pm
Excellent, mainly Mediterranean cooking, and a menu that varies daily: mullet grilled in tomato and tarragon sauce; lamb kebab with a cold mint, coriander, cucumber and chili sauce; spare ribs marinated in lemon with dried tomato and rosemary butter; and Flemish beef in Belgian beer with a puree of

apples, potatoes and plums. In summer the dining room opens onto a small inner patio. À la carte 25–30 €.

Take Thai (D D3)
→ *Utrechtsestraat 87*
Tel. 622 05 77
Daily 6–10.30pm
A very fashionable Thai restaurant with a basic, minimalist white decor, that won't distract you from what's in your plate: authentic, delicious Thai food. Popular so reserve ahead. À la carte 28–30 €.

Zushi (D C1)
→ *Amstel 20*
Tel. 330 68 82
Daily noon–11pm
In the center of the room, the *sushiman* prepares and serves *sushi, temaki, sashimi* and *tepanyaki*. The plates pass on a conveyor belt, in front of you – reach out and help yourself to anything you fancy. Fast, healthy eating. No reservations. Dishes from 25 €.

CAFÉS, COFFEESHOP

Café-restaurant Moko (D D3)
→ *Amstelveld 12*
www.goodfoodgroup.nl
Tel. 626 11 99
Daily 11.30am–11pm
Closed Mon in winter

BACKSTAGE

MULLIGANS

CONCERTO

Café adjoining the wooden Amstel church. Particularly inviting in fine weather, when the beautiful terrace on the church square can be fully enjoyed.

Backstage (D D3)

→ Utrechtsedwarsstraat 67
Tel. 622 36 38
Mon-Sat 10am–5.30pm
The regulars still call it the Backstage Twins. Greg is not there any more, leaving Gary as the only twin remaining of the former disco stars the Christmas Twins. The spirit of the place has not changed though, nor has the startling decor with its bedazzling array of colors. Not an inch of the walls, floors, tables or benches have remained unscathed by the creative fancy of the owners, who have left part of their soul into every nook and cranny of this inimitable dive. Hanging overhead are sweaters, hats and gaudy dresses knitted by one of the Twins. Drink outside in summer, among flower pots and scrap-iron sculptures.

De Huyschkaemer (D D3)

→ Utrechtsestraat 137
Tel. 627 05 75
Sun-Thu 5pm–1am;
Fri-Sat 5pm–3am
Huyschkammer means

'living room'. It is indeed the atmosphere created by this cozy, small, split-level café-restaurant with mosaic floors. DJs add to the excitement on Friday and Saturday nights (depending on the week). Mixed, easy-going clientele.

Brasserie Schiller (D C2)

→ Rembrandtplein 26–36
Tel. 554 07 23
Daily 7am–11pm
The epitome of Art Deco, this traditional café-restaurant dates from 1912. Eat on the terrace, or in the Portrait Room, surrounded by the 'Between Lunch and Dinner' series of paintings by Fritz Schiller, the businessman and part-time artist who imbued the place with the spirit that is still palpable today. The best destination for coffee, lunch or dinner in Rembrandtplein.

Rokerij III (D C1)

→ Amstel 8
Tel. 620 04 84
www.rokerij.net
Daily 9am–1am
The third Rokerij coffeeshop boasts mind-blowing decoration; the menu promises connoisseurs a similar experience. Well-informed staff and a very laid-back

atmosphere. Other branches include Lange Leidsedwarsstraat 41 (the first Rokerij coffeeshop – a gem) and Singel 8.

PUB, NIGHTCLUBS

Mulligan's (D D1)

→ Amstel 100
Tel. 622 13 30 Mon-Fri 3.30pm–1am; Sat-Sun 2.30pm–1am (3am Sat)
The most authentic Irish pub in Amsterdam. Live traditional Irish music (Wed-Sun 10pm).

Escape (D C2)

→ Rembrandtplein 11
Tel. 622 11 11 Thu-Sun 11pm–4am (7am Fri-Sat)
www.escape.nl
The most popular house and techno club in the city, and the largest, too, with a capacity of well over 2,000 people. Local and international stars stand at the turntables, but on Friday and Saturday nights, from 11pm, the spectacular Chemistry@Escape sets the house on fire. Sometimes open at the beginning of the week.

De Duivel (D C2)

→ Reguliersdwarsstraat 87
Tel. 626 61 84 Daily 8pm–3am (4am Fri-Sat)
Lively hip-hop bar. DJs, funk and rare groove evenings.

SHOPPING

Famous (D D3)

→ Huidenstraat 17
Tel. 528 67 06 Tue-Sun 11am–6pm (5pm Sat-Sun)
Signed photos of James Brown, a tennis ball signed by Monica Seles, Bruce Willis's baseball cap, etc.; the range of authenticated articles is vast and worth a visit. Also available, limited editions of gold records, Swatch watches designed by Sam Francis...

Concerto (D D3)

→ Utrechtsestraat 52–60
Tel. 623 52 28
Mon-Sat 10am–6pm (9pm Thu); Sun 10am–6pm
New and secondhand CDs and vinyl, covering a host of musical styles (classical, jazz, reggae, funk, etc.). Take time to browse: this is a haven for rare treasures if not latest hits.

Holland Gallery De Munt (D C1)

→ Muntplein 12
Tel. 623 22 71
Mon-Sat 10am–6pm
If you can't resist one of the typical delftware souvenirs, then buy it from this shop, the specialist in Delft and Makkum earthenware since 1890. You will find here what you need. Pieces from 50 €–5,000 €. Situated in the Mint Tower.

1 Map 1

KONINKLIJK THEATER CARRÉ ★

MAGERE-
BRUG ★

NIEMEYER-
MUSEUM

AMSTELHOF

MUSEUM WILLET-
HOLTHUYSEN

BLAUW-
BRUG

JOODS
HISTORISCH
MUSEUM

HORTUS BOTANICUS

PORTUGEES SYNAGOGE

MOZES-EN AARONKERK

MUZIEK-
THEATER

STOPERA

STADHUIS

NIEUWE ACHTERGRACHT

NIEUWE ACHTERGRACHT

NIEUWE PRINSEN-GRACHT

NIEUWE PRINSEN-GRACHT

PRINSENGRACHT

PRINSENGRACHT

WEESPERSTRAAT

KEIZERSGRACHT

KEIZERSGRACHT

NIEUWE KEIZERSGRACHT

NIEUWE KEIZERSGRACHT

NIEUWE HERENGRACHT

NIEUWE HERENGRACHT

UTRECHTSESTRAAT

UTRECHTSESTRAAT

MUIDER-STRAAT

HERENGRACHT

AMSTEL

AMSTEL

AMSTEL

BINNEN-

AMSTELSTRAAT

BINNENAMSTEL

BINNENAMSTEL

NIEUWE AMSTELSTRAAT

J.D. Meijer
plein

Waterloo-
plein

WATERLOO-
PLEIN

Mr. Visser-
plein

Waterloo-
plein

ZWANENBURGWAL

ZWANENBURGWAL

BURGWAL

MUSEUM WILLET-HOLTHUYSEN

REMBRANDTPLEIN

SARPHATISTRAAT
GRACHT
M.J. KOSTERSTRAAT
AMSTEL
Frederiks-plein
HOGESLUIS-BRUG
Professor Tupplein
SARPHATISTRAAT
SARPHATISTRAAT
SARPHATIKADE
ACHTER OOSTEINDE
OOSTEINDE
WESTEINDE
SARPHATIKADE
TORONTO-BRUG
SINGEL-GRACHT
HUDDEKADE
MAURITSKADE
SINGEL-GRACHT
SWAMMERDAMSTR.
WEESPERZIJDE
SINGEL-GRACHT
STADHOUDERSKADE
AMSTELDIJK
AMSTEL
WEESPERZIJDE
SKADE D
E
F

KONINKLIJK THEATER CARRÉ

he basement is a construction of an 18th-tury kitchen. The autiful French-style den can also be seen m Amstelstraat.

Museum **n Loon (D** C2)
Keizersgracht 672
624 52 55
Mon 11am–5pm
Van Loon family (co-nders of the East India mpany) was the last one ccupy this palatial ding. As the Calvinist losophy forbade any nting of wealth, only a npse inside this house convey the degree of lence in which the

Amstel bourgeoisie used to live. In the suite of Louis XV salons and apartments, family portraits, old masters and trompe-l'œil paintings lead to a French-style garden, typical of canal-side residences. At the back lies the old carriage shed.

★ **Reguliersgracht (D** C2)
This charming canal, bored in 1664, owes its name to the convent of *regular* nuns that used to stand nearby before the construction of the canal network. The top of Herengracht provides one of Amsterdam's most famous views: the beautiful perspective

of the row of seven bridges straddling the canal.

★ **Magere Brug (D** E2)
This delicate construction, made of exotic wood, is undoubtedly the most famous landmark in the city. Built in 1671, the 'thin bridge' has been widened and overhauled several times, but it is still opened by hand to make way for the barges on the Amstel. Upstream of the bridge lies the Blauwbrug ('blue bridge'), built for the International Exhibition in 1883, and downstream the Amstelsluizen, 17th-century wooden sluices that made it possible to replace

the canal water, can still be seen.

★ **Koninklijk Theater Carré (D** E3)
→ Amstel 115–125
Tel. 0900 25 25 255
Guided backstage tours
Wed and Sat 3pm
Just opposite the sluices, the huge façade of the Carré Theater, based on classical models, is decorated with the heads of clowns and jesters. Originally designed to house the circus of Oscar Carré (1887), the building then became the city's principal showcase for Italian opera. These days its program is more varied.

VAN GOGH MUSEUM

RIJKSMUSEUM

★ Vondelpark (E A1)

Named after Joost van der Vondel, a major 17th-century poet, this is a wonderful English-style park, with over 100 types of trees. Throughout the year skaters, cyclists and walkers of all ages follow the asphalt paths between the lush lawns, ponds and fountains. Free summer concerts in the Openlucht-theater.

★ Filmmuseum (E A1)

→ Vondelpark 3
Tel. 589 14 00 Check for times: www.filmmuseum.nl
A major movie theater occupies the white pavilion to the northeast of the park. A thousand movies are shown here every year, along with live musical accompaniment for silent movies. Open-air screenings in summer.

★ Hollandse Manege (E A1)

→ Vondelstraat 140
Tel. 618 09 42 Mon-Tue, Thu-Fri 2pm–midnight; Wed 10am–midnight; Sat-Sun 10am–5pm
A surprising discovery, on the corner of Vondelstraat: the Dutch riding school, a neoclassical building inspired by Vienna's Spanish Riding School. The Royal Riding School was founded in 1882 and had then as many as 143 stalls. Today it is still very active.

★ Van Gogh Museum (E B2)

→ Paulus Potterstraat 7
www.vangoghmuseum.nl
Tel. 570 52 00 Daily 10am–6pm (10pm Fri). Closed Jan 1
Almost the entire œuvre of Van Gogh is assembled in this unique museum, from the Potato Eaters to the unmistakable Cornfield with Crows. A total of 200 paintings and 550,000 drawings, spread over three floors, classified both thematically and chronologically. Also on show are paintings by Van Gogh's contemporaries: Gauguin, Toulouse-Lautrec, Monet...

★ Rijksmuseum (E C

→ Stadhouderskade 42
Tel. 674 70 47
www.rijksmuseum.nl
Daily 9am–6pm. Closed J
Due to extensive refurbish
galleries will be only part
open until 2008
Built to house the natio
collections, the Rijksmu
quickly grew into one o
world's greatest museu
1.2 million visitors per y
200 galleries, 800,000
drawings, 5,000 paintin
bona fide masterpieces
The Night Watch, The Je
Bride (Rembrandt), The
Milkmaid, Woman Read
A Letter (Vermeer), The
Merry Drinker (Franz Ha

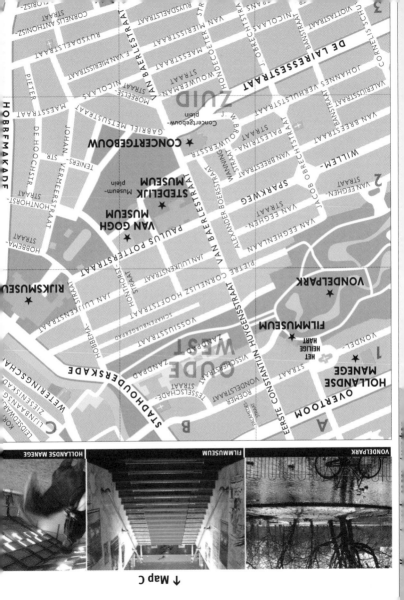

↓ Map C

To the south of Stadhouderskade lies Museumplein, the district that houses the Rijksmuseum, Van Gogh Museum and Stedelijk Museum. Luxury stores and top designers hold court on P.C.Hoofstraat and Van Baerlestraat, while the private hotels and middle-class houses around Vondelpark enjoy an enviable calm. Southeast, in contrast, De Pijp, a multicultural and student district with a proud working-class history, teems with exotic restaurants and inviting cafés. Beyond the Amstelkanal lies the South Plan, a housing estate designed by architects and city planners of the Amsterdam School.

RENZO'S

RESTAURANTS

Renzo's (E B3)
→ *Van Baerlestraat 67*
Tel. 673 16 73
Mon-Fri 10am–10pm;
Sat-Sun 11am–7pm
Renzo's is not really a restaurant but a homely deli. You can sit on big cushions in the main room or the mezzanine, before trying the ready-prepared dishes on display in the window. Just looking at them makes the mouth water: meat, vegetables, spaghetti in squid ink, paella, etc. You can sit outside in the summer.
À la carte 10–15 €.

Siempre Tapas (E E2)
→ *1ˢᵗ Sweelinckstraat 23*
Tel. 671 86 16
Daily 5–10.30pm
An ideal stop after a tour of the Albert Cuyp market. This tiny, very quaint café decorated with wood furniture, white and navy blue tiles, has a large selection of genuinely good tapas and other very tasty Spanish dishes. Take a seat near the fireplace or, in summer, on the beautiful terrace. Fun, friendly atmosphere and crowded with locals in the evening.
À la carte 14 €.

Stof (E E3)
→ *Van der Helstplein 9*
Tel. 364 03 54
Daily 6–10pm
A cozy restaurant in a lovely square where the tables are adorned with candles and tulips. The inventive cooking is based on seasonal ingredients: chicken marinated in mustard and brandy, lamb in honey and thyme sauce, zander fillet with shrimps. Convivial and welcoming. À la carte 25 €.

Pulpo (E A2)
→ *Willemsparkweg 87*
Tel. 676 07 00 Mon-Sat
noon–3pm, 5.30–10pm
International cooking with a strong Mediterranean influence is served here, with a varied menu of meat, fish and vegetarian dishes. The restaurant is elegant and the decoration somewhat understated. Ask for a table with a view over the inner garden, or one on the terrace in summer. À la carte 25 €.

De Ondeugd (E D2)
→ *Ferdinand Bolstraat 13*
Tel. 672 06 51 Daily 6–11pm
www.ondeugd.nl
Elaborate cooking but, above all, an interior worthy of a nightclub. The walls are covered with luminous motifs, there are mirror balls on the ceiling

PRE TAPAS

DE ONDEUGD

COBRA

and chandeliers are fitted with strange light bulbs. The menu is an inspired marriage of tradition and fantasy: scallops with champagne and curry sauce, duck with orange and Turkish fig fritters, crème brûlée with saffron. Astonishing private dining room. Fashionable clientele; reservation is necessary. À la carte 25–35 €.

L'Angoletto (E F2)
→ Hemonystraat 18
Tel. 676 41 82
Sun-Fri 6–11.30pm
One of the best Italian restaurants in Amsterdam, L'Angoletto stands at the corner of a small back street in the De Pijp area. Its steamed-up windows herald the crush that lies within as the cookers, separated from the dining room by only a counter, diffuse their aromas over the big shared tables. Friendly family setting and genuine Italian cooking. It may take a while for your food to arrive but you'll find it was worth the wait À la carte 25–30 €.

CAFÉS, COFFEESHOP

Vertigo (E A1)
→ Vondelpark 3
Tel. 612 30 21

www.vertigo.nl
Daily 10am–1am (11am Mon-Fri in Oct-March)
The terrace of the bar-restaurant Vertigo is arguably the most beautiful in Amsterdam. It is at the foot of the Filmuseum and offers wonderful views of the Vondelpark, with its parade of roller skaters and pedestrians. Excellent choice of beers.

Cobra (E C2)
→ Hobbemastraat 18
Tel. 470 01 11
www.cobracafe.nl
Daily 10am–10pm
In summer this spacious steel and glass café puts around 200 chairs out onto the esplanade of the museums, to the great delight of visitors. The interior is the realm of artists from the CoBra movement – even the plates are decorated.

Brandmeester's (E B3)
→ Van Baerlestraat 13
Tel. 675 78 88
Mon-Sat 9am–6pm (5pm Sat); Sun noon–5pm
Fresh coffee, roasted daily, to take out or drink on-site. The menu also offers teas, brownies, muffins, apple pies, etc.

Yo-Yo (E F2)
→ 2st Jan van der Heijdenstraat 79

Tel. 664 71 73
Daily noon–7pm
Just a short walk from the lesser-known Sarphati Park, Yo-Yo is slightly cheaper and considerably quieter (on the boring side of quiet, some would say) than the coffeeshops in the center. As elsewhere, friendly and helpful staff. Snacks, 'organic herb'.

Bakkerswinkel van Nineties (E C3)
→ Roelof Hartstraat 68
Tel. 662 35 94
Tue-Sat 7am–6pm (5pm Sat); Sun 10am–4pm
Very popular bakery (at the front)-cum-tearoom (at the back), which is renowned for the quality and freshness of its products. It has an extensive snack menu; excellent teas and coffees. Always packed.

BARS, CONCERT VENUES, THEATER

Kingfisher (E D2)
→ Ferdinand Bolstraat 24
Tel. 671 23 95
Mon-Sat 11am–1am (3am Fri-Sat)
A charming café with subdued lighting. Packed with young locals in the evenings.

Carel's Café (E D2)
→ Frans Halsstraat 76

Tel. 679 48 36
Mon-Sat 10am–1am (3am Fri-Sat); Sun 11am–1am
A large café with wood paneling and garlands of lights, tucked away in a quiet street. Do not be deceived by the relaxed calm in the day – at night it bursts into life. Tacos and simple dishes prepared on the spot are served at the bar.

De Badcuyp (E E2)
→ 1e Sweelinckstraat 10
Tel. 675 96 69
www.badcuyp.nl
Tue-Sun 11am–1am
Once the municipal swimming pool, now a cultural center with a varied program, including didgeridoo concerts, readings, plays, Brazilian parties, workshops, etc. Admission can be free or not, depending on the event.

SHOPPING

Betsy Palmer (E F3)
→ Van Woustraat 46
Tel. 470 97 95
www.betsypalmer.com
Mon noon–6pm; Tue-Sat 10am–6pm (5pm Sat)
Smartly designed store with a soft pastel interior, selling fashionable women's shoes in unusual colors.

STEDELIJK MUSEUM

ERGEBOUW

BERU...

3

OSTADESTRAAT

SARPHATIPARK

HEIDENSTRAAT

JAN VAN DER

CEINTUURBAN

VAN WOUST...

2e SWEELINCKSTR. SARPHATIPARK

2e JAN VAN DER HEIDENSTR.

STEENSTRAAT

e JAN STEEN-STRAAT

FLINCKSTRAAT

CUYPSTRAAT

ERT

ARD DOUSTR

REDAMSTRAAT

SARPHATI
PARK

★

ALBERT
CUYPMARKT

★
ALBERT CUYPSTRAAT

GERARD

DOUSTRAAT

BOLSTRAAT

GERARD

D STAPERL-
STRAAT

ALPERTISTRAAT

JELLIJNSTRAAT

2e JAN

STEENSTRAAT

HEMONYSTRAAT

VAN WOUST...

STEENSTRAAT

FLINCKSTRAAT

HEMONYLAAN

HEINEKEN
BROUWERIJ

★

2e JACOB VAN CAMPENSTRAAT

JACOB VAN
AMPENSTRAAT

FRANS
HALSSTR.

STADHOUDERSKADE

2

STADHOUDERSKADE

STADHOUDERSKADE

SINGELGRACHT

NICOLAAS WITSENKADE

WITSEN
STR.

DEN TEXSTRAAT

WETERING-
PLANTSOEN

SARPHATISTRAAT

WESTEINDE

OOSTEINDE

WETERINGSCHANS

WETERINGSCHANS

TERINGSCHANS

RACHT

VIJZELGRACHT

LIJNBAANSGRACHT

LIJNBAANSGRACHT

FOKKE SIMONSZSTRAAT

NIEUWE LOOIERSSTRAAT

NOORDERSTRAAT

NBAANSGRACHT

WETERINGDWARSSTR.

1e WETERINGDWARSSTRAAT

2e WETERINGDWARSSTRAAT

HUIDEKOPERSTRAAT

WETERINGSCHANS

WETERINGSCHANS

WETERINGSCHANS

FALK-
STRAAT

DE DUIF
KERK

REGULIERSGRACHT

REGULIERSGRACHT

REGULIERSGRACHT

PRINSENGRACHT

PRINSENGRACHT

PRINSENGRACHT

PRINSENGRACHT

PRINSENGRACHT

PRINSENGRACHT

KERKSTRAAT

KERKSTRAAT

Amstelveld

AMSTELKERK

+

Frederiks-
plein

M.J.
KOSTERSTR

ACHTER-
GRACHT

1

UTRECHTSEDWARSSTR

PRINSEN-
GRACHT

PRINSENGRACHT

AMSTEL

UTRECHTSESTRAAT

UTRECHTSEDWARS-
STRAAT

KER...
STRAAT

F

E

D

HEINEKEN BROUWERIJ

SARPHATIPARK

ALBERT-CUYPMARKT

...ot overlook the
...aordinary 18th-century
...houses.

...tedelijk
...seum (E B2)
...aulus Potterstraat 13
...73 29 11 www.stedelijk.nl
... 10am–6pm (9pm Thu).
...ed Jan 1

... of the most diverse
...ern art collections in
... world (photographs,
...tings , sculptures,
...allations and
...ormances) and some 30
..., focusing on the avant-
...e. The permanent
...ction is especially well
...esented in summer.
...t miss: Mondrian,

Malevich, the CoBra group.

★ Heineken Brouwerij (E D2)
→ Stadhouderskade 78
Tel. 523 96 66
www.heinekenexperience.com
Tue–Sun 10am–6pm (final
admission 5pm). Closed Dec
25 and Jan 1; under-18s must
be accompanied by an adult
Guided tour of the former
Heineken factory (1934),
with breweries dominated
by enormous copper vats
and stables containing the
carts that were used for
deliveries. Free beer tasting.

★ Concertgebouw (E B2)
→ Concertgebouwplein 2–6
Tel. 671 83 45
www.concertgebouw.nl

Daily 10am–5pm
The Concertgebouw, built
on the initiative of music-
loving private citizens
anxious to heighten the
city's profile, now draws
over 800,000 people every
year. Its orchestra has a
worldwide reputation.The
Grote Zaal ('large hall'),
based on the Felix Meritis
Theater, is renowned for its
excellent acoustics.

★ Albert-Cuypmarkt (E E2)
→ Albert Cuypstraat
between Ferdinand Bolstraat
and Van Woustraat
www.albertcuypmarkt.com
Mon–Sat 9am–6pm
Amsterdam's biggest

market has been the pulsing
heart of De Pijp for almost
a century. Nearly 2 miles of
fruit, flowers, vegetables,
meat, fish, clothes and
knickknacks. A host of
exotic goods, reflecting the
area's multiculturalism.
Small restaurants and
friendly cafés in the
adjoining streets.

★ Sarphatipark (E E3)
Charming English-style park,
the green lung of
the Pijp. In the center,
a monument has been
erected in honor of Sarphati
(1813–66), the instigator
of many social projects in
this working-class
neighborhood.

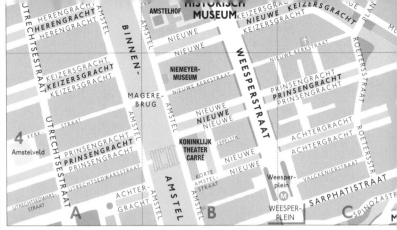

VERZETSMUSEUM

ZOO ARTIS

★ Museum Het Rembrandthuis (F A2)

→ Jodenbreestraat 4–6
Tel. 520 04 00
www.rembrandthuis.nl
Mon-Sat 10am–5pm;
Sun and public hols 1–5pm.
Closed Jan 1

It was in this house, acquired in 1639 thanks to the private fortune of his wife Saskia, that Rembrandt spent his most glorious years. By 1658 he had fallen into disgrace and was forced to sell everything. The modern inventory of his assets has made it possible to reconstruct the interior and capture the atmosphere in which the great master lived, worked and taught. The museum houses 250 of his etchings.

★ Portugees Synagoge (F B3)

→ Mr Visserplein 3
Tel. 624 53 51
Sun-Fri 10am–4pm.
Closed for Yom Kippur

A treasure from 1675, kept intact for over 300 years. It owes its name to the Jews who emigrated to Amsterdam via Portugal after they were expelled from Spain. Brick walls studded with 72 windows; copper chandeliers groaning with 1,000 candles; an imposing hechal (Torah closet),

made of jacaranda...

★ Hortus Botanicus (F C3)

→ Plantage Middenlaan 2A
Tel. 625 84 11
Mon-Fri 9am–5pm (9pm July-Aug); Sat-Sun and public hols 10am–5pm (9pm July-Aug).
Closed Jan 1, Dec 25

Doctors were the first to cultivate the plants brought back by Dutch sailors in the 17th century. The greenhouses of the old Hortus Medicis (1682) are still fascinating today. Legend has it that several species were propagated around the world thanks to specimens from this garden: coffee, for example, found

its way to America via plants brought from Afri

★ Nationaal Vakbondsmuseum (F

→ Henri Polaklaan 9
Tel. 624 11 66
Tue-Fri 11am–5pm; Sun 1–5pm. Closed public hols

The former HQ of the diamond worker's union now a trade union museum, is Berlage's m accomplished building. Its austere brick facade evokes the power of the union. Inside, an impos stairwell rises up into th light pouring through the glass roof. The lamp in the form of diamonds pay tribute to the diamc

HOLLANDSCHE SCHOUWBURG

HORTUS ... GUS

PORTUGEES SYNAGOGE

NIEUWE AMSTELSTRAAT

AMSTEL

BI AMV

AMSTEL

BINNEN AMSTEL

MUIDER- STRAAT

NIEUWE HERENGRACHT

Jonas Daniël Meijerplein

MUZIEK- THEATER

Waterloo-M. plein

STOPERA

OPERA

H POLAKL

WERTHEIM- PARK

WATERLOO- PLEIN

Mr. Visser- plein

STADHUIS

MUSEUM HET REMBRANDTHUIS

NATION VAKBONDS

RAPENBURGERSTRAAT

NIEUWE HERENGRACHT

VALKENBURGERSTRAAT

JODENBREESTR

GROENBURGWAL

ZWANENBURGWAL

KLOVENIERSBURGWAL

ENTE...

A TRANSTRAAT

VALKENBURGERSTRAAT

MOZES-EN AäRONKERK

NIEUWE UILENBURGERSTRAAT

JDN HOUTTUINEN

NIEUWE ST-ANTONIESBREESTRAAT

ZUIDERKERK

KLOVENIERSBURGWAL

RAAMGRACHT

RUSLAND

RAPENBURGERSTR.

NIEUWE UILENBURGERGRACHT

OUDESCHANS

HOUT- KOPERS- BURGWAL

HOOGSTR

OUDE HOOGSTR

Rapenburger- plein

NIEUWMARKT

FOELIEDWARSSTR

FOELIESTR.

RAPENBURG...STR

OUDESCHANS

OUDESCHANS

KROMBOOMSSLOOT

NIEUW MARKT

BETHANIEN-STR.

OUDEKERKSTR

PRINS

PRINS H TUN

PEPERSTR.

'S GRAVEN- HEKJE

OOSTER- SEKADE

OUDESCHANS

MONTELBAANSTOREN

NIEUW MARKT

RECHT BOOMSSLOOT

KONINGS STR.

'S GRAVEN- HEKJE

'SGRAVEN- HEKJE

'GRANDE- STEEG

OUDEZIJDS VOORBURGWAL

Nieuw Markt

WAAG

BLOED- STR.

BINNENKANT

WAALSKANT

KALK- MARKT

EILANDSGRACHT

OUDE WAAL

KROMME WAAL

NIEUWE- STR.

NIEUWE JONKER-STR.

NIEUWE BINNEN WAAL

CENTRUM

OUDEZIJDS VOORBURGWAL

OOSTERDOK

PRINS HENDRIKKADE

SCHEEPVAARTHUIS

GELDERSEKADE

GELDERSEKADE

GELDERSEKADE

GELDERSEKADE

GELDERSEKADE

ZEEDIJK

KROMME WAAG

ZEEDIJK

TEMPLE HE HWA

OUDE KERK

WARMOESSTRAAT

Oudekerks- plein

VOORBURGWAL

MUSEUM AMSTELKRING

DAMRAK

OOSTERDOK

OOSTBOK-

BSTERDOK

C

↑ Map A

The five synagogues located around Waterlooplein are the most visible traces of Amsterdam's old Jewish Quarter, which was heavily damaged during World War Two and then partially demolished for the construction of the subway. Plantage, a bourgeois district dotted with large green areas (hence its name), is home to the zoo and the botanical garden. Further north, the old port district is a quiet haven set away from the hustle and bustle of the city center. Be sure to take a stroll down the Entrepotdok, a quay flanked by a row of 82 former maritime warehouses (1827–40) that have been magnificently restored.

DE DRUIF

EIK & LINDE

RESTAURANTS

Koffiehuis van de Volksbond (F D2)
→ *Kadijksplein 4*
Tel. 622 12 09
Daily 5.30–10pm
At the north end of Entrepotdok, the erstwhile 'coffee house' for dockers is now a popular restaurant, with huge meals at incredibly good prices. You may have to share your table with strangers if you're not occupying all the seats. À la carte 17 €.

Kilimanjaro (F C2)
→ *Rapenburgerplein 6*
Tel. 622 34 85
Tue-Sun 5–10pm
The menu of this unpretentious and friendly restaurant offers a crash tour of African cuisine, from Tunisia to South Africa via Cabo Verde and Ethiopia, with particular emphasis on specialties from the latter, and its neighbor, Eritrea. African wines, beers and cocktails. À la carte 20–30 €.

Hemelse Modder (F B1)
→ *Oude Waal 9*
Tel. 624 32 03
Daily 6–10pm
Modern and inviting restaurant serving a mixture of French and Italian cuisine. There's a wide range of starters, meat, fish, vegetarian dishes and desserts on offer. The crowning glory is the chocolate mousse (the 'heavenly mud' that gives this restaurant its name). Reservations advisable. À la carte 26 €.

CAFÉS, COFFEESHOP

Dantzig (F A3)
→ *Zwanenburgwal 15*
Tel. 620 90 39
Mon-Sat 9am–1am (3am Sat); Sun 10am–1am
Ideal for a breather before or after a visit to the nearby flea market, the Dantzig resembles a big library, with bookshelves and vast reading tables. The large terrace, facing the controversial Stopera building, home to the city hall and the opera house, offers unrestricted views of the Amstel and the Muntorren. Great vibe.

Greenhouse Namaste (F B3)
→ *Waterlooplein 345*
Tel. 622 54 99 Daily 9am–1am (2am Fri-Sat)
www.greenhouse.org
This is the smallest of the Greenhouse coffeeshops and it maintains the high standards of decoration. The Greenhouse

E SLUYSWACHT   WATERLOOPLEINMARKT   HET FORT VAN SJAKOO

reputation, however, rests on the cafés' successive victories in the prestigious High Times Cup (1993–9), as well as the various prizes awarded in the Cannabis Cup. Other branch: Oude Zijdsvoorburgwal 191.

Eik & Linde (F C3)
→ Plantage Middenlaan 22
Tel. 622 57 16
Mon-Fri 11am–1am (2am Fri); Sat 2pm–2am
Highly enjoyable, archetypal Dutch brown bar dating to 1858. Tourist-free and a neighborhood favorite, it has friendly, very relaxed surroundings; the place really starts to fill up in the early evening. Very good beers.

De Druif (F C2)
→ Rapenburgerplein 83
Tel. 624 45 30
Mon-Sat noon–1am (2am Fri-Sat); Sun 1pm–1am
'The Grape' is a genuine brown café, with the obligatory coating of nicotine on the walls and a pleasant location in the old port neighborhood. Most of the customers are locals. More wine than beer is served here.

Café de Sluyswacht (F A2)
→ Jodenbreestraat 1
www.welcome.to/sluyswacht
Tel. 625 76 11

Mon-Sat 10am–1am (3am Fri-Sat); Sun 11am–7pm
Set in a narrow lock keeper's house that is now almost 300 years old. Its large terrace on the banks of the Oudeschans is not to be missed in good weather.

Brouwerij 't IJ (F F3)
→ Funenkade 7
Tel. 622 83 25
www.brouwerijhetij.nl
Wed-Sun 3–7.45pm
This café, set in a windmill, brews its own beer (which bears the same name). Tourists are rare but locals pack this narrow place as soon as the doors open, standing and drinking around the bar.

BARS, CONCERT VENUES, THEATER

De Kluis (F C2)
→ Prins Hendrikkade 194
Tel. 622 48 09
www.lasergames.nl
A nightspot specializing in Latin music, just opposite the NeMo. Popular Brazilian music – Forro (Tuesday), salsa (Wednesday, Friday) and jazz jam sessions (Thursday). Don't miss the Big Brazilian Party (twice a month on Saturday), with DJs and

live groups unleashing their irresistible rhythms. Admission 2 €.

Bimhuis (F B2)
→ Oudeschans 73–77
Tel. 623 13 61
www.bimhuis.nl
Thu-Sun from 9pm.
Closed July-Aug
Amsterdam's most important jazz venue, featuring musicians from all over the world. Reserve in advance.

Tropeninstituut Theater (F E4)
→ Mauritskade 63 and Linnaeusstraat 2
Tel. 568 87 11,
www.kit.nl/theater
Conferences, movies, dance, world music – the Tropeninstituut's program is very extensive. All year round Latin Dance Party, African Dance Party and Tango Tanz Salon nights.

Hotel Arena Tonight (F D4)
→ Gravesandestraat 51
Tel. 694 74 44
www.hotelarena.nl
A small lively club, with a crowd aged 20–30, in the hotel of the same name. Dance, house and other electronic music. Salsa Lounge evening once a month (5pm). Café Todrink (open daily noon–midnight):

background music and pleasant terrace.

SHOPPING

Waterloopleinmarkt (F B3)
→ Waterlooplein
Mon-Sat 9am–5pm
The biggest and the oldest of the city's flea markets, which was already serving the local Jewish community two centuries ago. Everything you can imagine for sale: second-hand clothes, Indonesian fabrics, African crafts, books, records, shoes...

Het Fort van Sjakoo (F B2)
→ Jodenbreestraat 24
Tel. 625 89 79 Mon-Fri 11am–6pm (5pm Sat)
www.xs4all.nl/~sjakoo
An extraordinary political bookstore, kept afloat by contributions from well-wishers. From the adventures of a black-leathered hoodlum Tintin to punk records from Eastern Europe, from a pirate radio manual to an ABC of squatters' rights – a vast range of books, essays, newspapers, pamphlets and magazines are available on anarchism, the anti-globalization movement and the punk philosophy.

NMUSEUM

NEDERLANDS SCHEEPVAARTMUSEUM

NEMO

rs, pioneers in the ggle for workers' rights.

erzetsmuseum (F D3)
→ *antage Kerklaan 61A*
:20 25 35 Tue-Fri 10am–
: Sat-Mon noon–5pm
xhilarating exhibition
handful of men and
en who opted to join
esistance during the
occupation (photos,
destine printing press,
recordings).

o Artis (F D3)
antage Kerklaan 38–40
23 34 00 Daily
-5pm (6pm May-Sep)
oldest zoo in Europe
3), laid out like a park
shady promenades.
ot miss the huge

aquarium, with 2,000
species of fresh and
seawater fish.

★ **Tropenmuseum (F** E4)
→ *Linnaeusstraat 2*
www.tropenmuseum.nl
Tel. 568 82 15 Daily
10am–5pm. Closed Dec 25,
Jan 1, April 30 and May 5
A rich and varied approach
to developing countries.
Audio-visual reconstructions
(villages, souks, markets),
thematic exhibitions (music,
development, ecology),
art and crafts. Museum for
children (aged 6–12).

★ **Nederlands (F** D2)
Scheepvaartmuseum
→ *Kattenburgerplein 1*
Tel. 523 22 22

www.scheepvaartmuseum.nl
Daily 10am–5pm; Oct-Jun
(outside school hols): closed
Mon. Closed Jan 1, April 30
and Dec 25
Holland's entire maritime
history stored in the old
Admiralty arsenal (1656).
Models, navigation
instruments, paintings,
sea charts... On the quay,
a faithful reproduction of
an East Indies Company
three-master, with its crew
in period costume.

★ **NeMo (F** C1)
→ *Oosterdok 2*
Tel. 0900 919 11 00
www.e-nemo.nl
Tue-Sun 10am–5pm (open
Mon during school hols).

Closed Jan 1, April 30, Dec 25
Games, laboratories and
workshops to prove that
discovering science and
technology can be fun.

★ **Joods Historisch**
Museum (F B3)
→ *Jonas D. Meijerplein 2-4*
Tel. 626 99 45
www.jhm.nl
Daily 11am–5pm.
Closed Yom Kippur
Cultural relics, photos
and documents illustrating
the lives and identities of
Amsterdam's Jews. The
museum occupies four
Ashkenazic synagogues
(dating from 1671 to 1752),
which were places of
worship until 1943.

RRIVING BY TRAIN

m London take the
rostar to Brussels, then
e Thalys to Amsterdam
. 08705 186 186 (Eurostar)
w.eurostar.com
w.raileurope.co.uk/thalys
alys.asp

ntraal Station
the heart of the city,
nins from the Dam.
Tel. 0900 92 92

RLINES

KLM (in the UK)
. 08705 074 074
Easyjet (from the UK)
w.easyjet.co.uk
. 08717 500 100
www.Cheapflights.com
www.Orbitz.com

CENTRAAL STATION

TAXIS

Taxi ranks
Centraal Station, Dam,
Muntplein and Leidse-
plein. No night fares.
Central office
→ Tel. 677 77 77 (24 hrs)

CARS

Driving is highly
inadvisable beyond
Singelgracht (innumerable
pedestrian crossings,
expensive and limited
parking, traffic jams) –
better to explore the
center on foot.
Parking
→ Daily 9am–midnight
(Sun noon). In the center:
3.20 €/hr
Parking cards
From Stadhuis and from
branches of the *Dienst
Stadstoezcht*, the city's
parking service. Tourist
card at 28.80 €/day,
80.60 €/three days.
Parking lots
Parkings P + R
Unsupervized parking lots
on the outskirts. 5.50 €/
day, including two public
transportation tickets.
Information and list of
parking lots available from
the tourist office. You can
also consult the following
website:
www.toamsterdam.nl/
Car pound
→ Daniel Goedkoopstr. 7–9
Tel. 553 03 33
Daily 24 hrs

FERRIES

Linking Centraal Station
with Amsterdam Noord.
No cars. Price: 1 €
→ Daily 24 hrs (every 5–10
mins). Landing stage behind
the station (quays 8–9)

m on houseboats) to
t. From 75 € (standard
m), 115 € (two-room
artment), 150 €
o rooms on houseboat).
tel Acacia (**B** B4)
Lindengracht 251
. 622 14 60
w.hotelacacia.nl
ce curtains, tapestries...
e cozy interior of the
acia is typical of the
uses in Jordaan. Fully
uipped apartments and
dios can also be rented
two houseboats
ored in front. From 80 €
he room) and 90–110 €
udio and houseboat for
ee nights minimum).
inston Hotel (**A** C3)
Warmoesstraat 129
. 623 13 80
w.winston.nl
the heart of the Red Light
strict, this hotel may be
ge and modern but it
rtainly has character. The
ace is a platform for the

exhibition of works by
contemporary artists, who
have also decorated 30 of
the rooms. Some bedrooms
are even 'sponsored', such
as the new Stolichnaya
Room (by the vodka brand)
and Timberland Room (by
the fashion retailer). Red
and green walls, black satin
bedspreads, cowhide rugs,
bright yellow decor... the
place is certainly unusual.
From 79–89 €.
Hotel Orlando (**D** E3)
→ Prinsengracht 1099
Tel. 638 69 15
Airy, beautiful rooms (oak
parquet, 19th-century
furniture, clever lighting)
in a glorious building
dating from 1688.
80–130 €.
The Bridge Hotel (**D** E3)
→ Amstel 107–111
Tel. 623 70 68
www.thebridgehotel.nl
A modern hotel with
pleasant rooms, on the east
bank of the Amstel, just

opposite the locks. From
85–98 € (all taxes incl.).
Hotel La Bohème (**C** B4)
→ Marnixstraat 415
Tel. 624 28 28 www.la-
boheme-amsterdam.com
Comfortable, modern
hotel, very well located
near Leidseplein. Warm,
youthful welcome in the
bar-reception, where the
staff let you check your
emails. Minimum stay of
three nights at the
weekend. From 100 €.
**The Greenhouse
Effect** (**A** C3)
→ Warmoesstraat 55
Tel. 624 49 74 www.the-
greenhouse-effect.com
Small hotel with character:
themed one- or two-
bedrooms – Jungle Book,
1001 Arabian Nights,
Turkish Delight, Red Light,
Canal View – all decorated
more tastefully than the
slightly tacky names could
lead you to think. Friendly
welcome. Adjoining is the

AIRPORT

Schiphol Airport
Eleven miles (18 km) to
the south of the city,
→ Tel. 794 08 00
→ www.Schiphol.nl

Links to city center
Train to Centraal Station
→ Every 7 mins (every
hour at night). Journey
time 20 mins. Price: 5.50
€ (return). www.ns.nl
Schipol travel taxi
→ Shared taxis 19 €
By taxi
Journey time 25–50 mins;
Price: up to 40 €
By bus
→ Line no. 370 or
→ KLM shuttles
Price: 10.50–12.50 €
Tel. 649 56 51

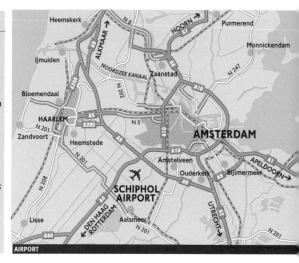

---

*Accommodation in
Amsterdam is pricey and
comfort is often reduced to
a strict minimum. Except
where otherwise
indicated, the prices given
are for a double room with
bathroom, in high season
(April to August), breakfast
included. Be prepared for
a key deposit of 10 € in
cash and a 5% tax, not
always included in the
price of the room. Payment
by credit card sometimes
entails a 6% surcharge.
Reservations are essential.*

APARTMENTS

**Amsterdam
Apartments (A** D3)
→ Kromme Waal 32
Tel. 626 59 30
Furnished studios and
apartments for rent from
one week (three nights
min. stay). Two persons:
from 50 € per night. Three
persons: from 45 €.

Youth hostels and cheap hotels

*Public youth hostels
(NJHC) offer reductions to
members. Private hostels
accept customers aged
between 18 and 35.*

**The Flying Pig Palace
Hostel (E** B1)
→ Vossiusstraat 46
Tel. 400 41 87
www.flyingpig.nl
The oldest of the two
Flying Pig hostels.
Both share the same
philosophy, but this one
is further from the city
center. However, it is
on the doorstep of the
Vondelpark and the
museums. Dorm. from
21.70 €/pers.

**The Flying Pig
Downtown Hostel (A** C2)
→ Nieuwendijk 100
Tel. 420 68 22
Both staff and guests
are seasoned travelers so
the atmosphere is young

and laid-back, without
skimping on cleanliness.
Free use of safe deposit
box. Access to kitchen.
The 'smokers' corner' is
inviting: low tables,
cushions and bay window.
Internet access. Dorm.
from 22.70 €/pers.

Groenendael (A B1)
→ Nieuwendijk 15
Tel. 624 48 22
A small hotel, 165 yards
from the railway station,
with basic comfort but
impeccable service. Some
rooms have en-suite
bathrooms. Breakfast is
served in a room lined
with foreign bank bills.
Excellent value for money.
From 50 €.

75–120 €

Hotel Bema (E B2)
→ Concertgebouwplein 19b
Tel. 679 13 96
www.bemahotel.com
A fine location in the

museum district.
Spacious, airy rooms (a
real luxury in Amsterdam)
The bathrooms, fitted with
skylights, are communal
but clean. Breakfast is
served in the room. From
75 € (with shower).

Hotel van Onna (B B5)
→ Bloemgracht 102–108
Tel. 626 25 77
www.hotelvanonna.com
This hotel has recently
been completely
refurbished. The rooms
are spotless, but the
prettiest are the five set up
in the attic. Good value for
money and very attentive
service. Reservations only
accepted by phone.
From 80 €.

**Amsterdam House
Hotel Eureka (A** C5)
→ 's-Gravelandseveer 3–4
Tel. 626 25 77
www.amsterdamhouse.com
Rooms and fully equipped
two- to five-bedroom
apartments (several of

Transport and hotels in Amsterdam

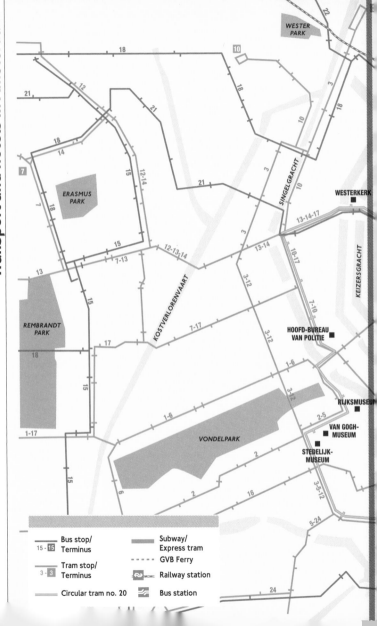

Bus stop/Terminus

15 - 15 **Tram stop/Terminus**

3 - 3

Circular tram no. 20

Subway/Express tram

GVB Ferry

Railway station

Bus station

WESTER PARK

ERASMUS PARK

REMBRANDT PARK

VONDELPARK

WESTERKERK

KEIZERSGRACHT

SINGELGRACHT

HOOFD-BUREAU VAN POLITIE

RIJKSMUSEUM

VAN GOGH-MUSEUM

STEDELIJK-MUSEUM

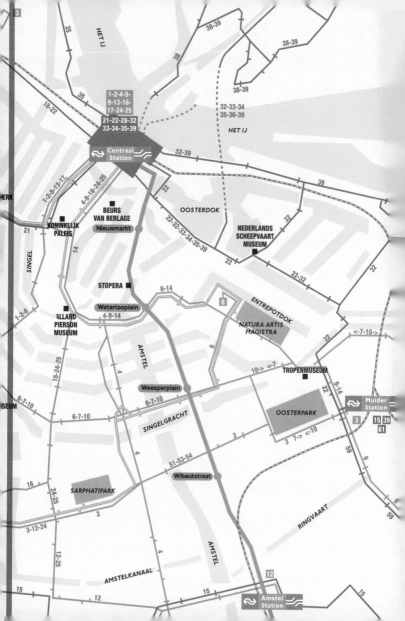

...est way to get
...d! Bicycle rental
...€/day, with ID
deposit.
...Bike (**C** A2)
...teringsschans 2
...28 76 88
...a bike
...straat (**A** B4)
...mstraat 20-22
...25 50 29
...9am–6pm
...éric Rent a
(**B** C4)
...ouwersgracht 78
...524 55 09
...v.frederic.nl
...9am–6pm
...owner also offers
...ns in his house
...–68 €).

...assade offers luxury
...hy of a palace and a
...feel: library, marble
...rooms, superbly
...orated 19th-century
...e bedrooms and lobby.
...–305 €.
...akfast 16 €.

...iller Hotel (D C2)
...embrandtplein 26-36
554 07 00
...w.nh-hotels.com
...s big Art Deco hotel is
...nous for its beautiful
...fé-restaurant. Ask for a
...om overlooking the
...uare. From 230 €.
...eakfast 16 €.

...ore than

...lakes (**C** C2)
...Keizersgracht 384
...el. 530 2010
...ww.blakesamsterdam.com
...ne brainchild of designer
...nouska Hempel, Blakes
...msterdam is, as its older
...ister Blakes London,
...a superb and skilful blend

of West and East with
Hempel's signature jet
black furniture. The
interiors of the 17th-
century canal-house are
so elegant, and doubtless
make it the most stylish
(and theatrical) place to
stay in Amsterdam. No
pastel or creme-beige
colors here: the 41 rooms
are each decorated in a
different group of striking
colors. The restaurant
(open to non guests) has
an Asian-inspired menu.
Exceptional service.
From 300 €.

Grand Hotel Sofitel Demeure (**A** B4)
→ Oudezijds
Voorburgwal 197
Tel. 555 31 11
www.thegrand.nl
The grandest hotel in town
and a building replete with
history; it was a 15th-
century convent, then a
16th-century 'Prinsenhof'
or royal residence, later a

19th-century city hall. Art
Nouveau interiors, marble,
Gobelins tapestries,
oriental rugs. The Café
Roux, decorated with a
fresco by Karel Appel, has
now been restored. From
420 €. Breakfast 25 €.

Hotel de l'Europe (**A** B5)
→ Nieuwe Doelenstraat 2–8
Tel. 531 17 77
www.leurope.nl
Majestic palace on the
banks of the Binnen
Amstel. The Excelsior
restaurant can be
reached by barge. 350 €.
Breakfast 22.50 €.

Crowne Plaza American (**C** B4)
→ Leidsekade 97
Tel. 556 30 00
The most famous of all the
city's hotels, with an Art
Deco façade classified as
a historic monument. So
is the Café Americain, one
of the most elegant cafés
in Europe. 335 €.
Breakfast 17.50 €.

The GVB runs the entire
public transport system.
Agency just in front of the
station.
→ Tel. 0900 400 40 40

Sales points
→ VVV, GVB agencies,
tobacconists, post offices,
newspaper sellers and
onboard (more expensive)
Travel cards valid for
trams, buses and subway.

Fares
Single tickets
→ 2.50 € (valid 1 ½ hrs)
Strippenkaart
→ 6.40 € (15-strip ticket)

Network
Divided into zones.
1 zone = 2 strips,
2 zones = 3 strips, etc.
The Centrum = 1 zone
(punch 2 strips)

Amsterdam Pass
→ 31 € (one day),
41 € (two days),
51 € (three days)
Access to all public
transport and to
25 museums, and one
free boat trip. Info and
tickets from the VVV.

Timetables
Subway, trams and
buses 6am–0.30am.

Tramway
17 lines. Most leave from
the central station.

Subway
Serves the outskirts,
especially Biljmer and
Amstelstation.

Buses
Run outside the ring
of canals.

Night lines
(midnight–6am)
→ Special ticket: 3 €
Usable on 12 bus
numbered 351 to 363.

Lost property
→ Tel. 0900 90 11

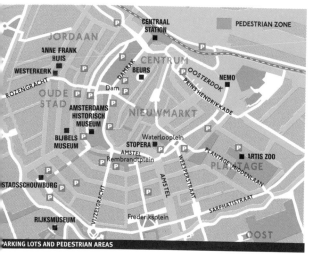

PEDESTRIAN ZONE

PARKING LOTS AND PEDESTRIAN AREAS

ponymous coffeeshop.
ar, disco. From 105 €.

**'an Ostade
Bicycle Hotel (E** E3)
→ Van Ostadestraat 123
el. 679 34 52
www.bicyclehotel.com
he façade of the Van
Ostade, decorated with
icycles, sets the tone of
he place. Here you can rent
he bikes, park them in the
overed garage and find all
he information, maps,
tc., that will make a two-
wheeled stay in Amsterdam
s enjoyable as possible. A
upplement payable when
aying by credit card.
rom 105 €.

20–190 €

Hotel Agora (C D3)
→ Singel 462
el. 627 22 00
ww.hotelagora.nl
lean and functional
otel in a very convenient
entral location, right next

to the flower market, on the
intersection of the main
tram lines and just a few
minutes from the flea
market, the city center and
the canals. 120–135 €.
Atlas Hotel (E A2)
→ Van Eeghenstraat 64
Tel. 676 63 36 www.ams.nl
In a residential street
flanked by private hotels.
The upper-story rooms
provide a side view of the
Vondelpark. From 129 €.
**Hotel Seven
Bridges (D** C2)
→ Reguliersgracht 31
Tel. 623 13 29
The hotel's name derives
from its view of seven
arched bridges. Marble,
plants and Biedermeier
style in the lobby. The eight
rooms are cozy (the higher
the floors, the smaller they
become) with dark parquet
floors, moldings on the
ceiling, Oriental rugs and
wooden furniture (one even
has a fireplace), and they

open onto the canal or the
inner garden. There are no
common areas, and that
means breakfast in bed!
A firm favorite with visitors
so reserve months ahead.
100–180 €.
't Hotel (B C5)
→ Leliegracht 18
Tel. 422 2741
www.thotel.nl
Renovated from a
traditional 17th-century
building by one of
Amsterdam's most
beautiful and romantic
canals, the 't Hotel has only
eight rooms. The style
inside is modern, elegant
and comfortable with a very
homely atmosphere.
Excellent buffet breakfast.
115–165 €.
Hotel de Filosoof
→ Anna Vondelstraat 6
Tel. 683 30 13
www.hotelfilosoof.nl
Set behind the Vondelpark,
De Filosoof is an invitation
not only to rest the body

but also to enrich the mir
each of the 38 room's
elegant decoration is bas
on a philosopher or
philosophical theme
(Buddha, Confucius,
Nietzsche, Wittgenstein,
etc.). Garden. 125–138 €.
Canal House Hotel (B C5
→ Keizersgracht 148
Tel. 622 51 82
www.canalhouse.nl
Luxurious hotel in three
adjoining houses dating
back to 1630, on the banks
of the canal in the Jordaan
area. The 26 rooms are
beautiful, decorated with
period furniture, floral
motifs and pastel colors.
The grand breakfast room
looks out on the inner
garden. A treat. 140–190 €.
Ambassade Hotel (C C2)
→ Herengracht 341
Tel. 555 02 22
www.ambassade-hotel.nl
Set in ten 17th-century
houses along the Singel and
the Herengracht, the